Python in Action: A Project-Based Introduction to Python Programming

Build Real-World Applications Step by Step

Andreas Braumann, Msc

"*Python in Action*" is an interactive, project-driven guide for beginners eager to dive into Python programming. This book takes a hands-on approach, focusing on learning by building real-world applications. From setting up your first Python project to creating fully functional programs, you will gain a solid understanding of Python's core concepts through practical exercises. Each chapter guides you through different projects, such as building a weather application, a to-do list, and even a simple game, making learning engaging and relevant. Whether you're new to programming or transitioning from another language, this book equips you with the skills needed to start coding confidently in Python.

Introduction   5
Chapter 1: Introduction to Python Programming   8

Chapter 2: Variables, Data Types, and Operations	14
Chapter 3: Control Flow and Loops	21
Chapter 4: Functions and Modular Code	28
Chapter 5: Working with Lists, Tuples, and Dictionaries	37
Chapter 8: Error Handling and Debugging	65
Chapter 11: Introduction to Regular Expressions (Regex)	93
Chapter 12: GUI Programming with Tkinter	104
Appendices	127

Introduction

Welcome to **Python in Action: A Project-Based Introduction to Python Programming**! Whether you're a complete beginner to programming or someone transitioning from another language, this book is designed to make your learning journey interactive, practical, and fun. Instead of relying solely on theory, we'll dive into the heart of Python by **building real-world projects** that demonstrate the power of the language.

Throughout the chapters, you'll work on hands-on projects that not only teach you Python but also introduce you to key programming concepts and problem-solving techniques. By the end of this book, you'll be well-equipped with the confidence and skills needed to start creating your own applications.

Here's what you'll learn as we progress through the book:

- **Python Fundamentals**: We start with the building blocks of Python—variables, data types, control flow (if/else statements), loops, and functions. You'll use these to write simple, yet powerful, scripts.
- **Object-Oriented Programming (OOP)**: Learn how to model real-world entities using Python's OOP capabilities. You'll understand how to create classes, objects, and how inheritance and encapsulation work in Python.
- **File Handling and Error Handling**: You'll explore how to read from and write to files, making your programs capable of handling external data. Additionally, you'll learn how to deal with exceptions and ensure your code runs smoothly, even in the face of errors.
- **Working with External Libraries**: Extend Python's power by integrating third-party libraries. We'll show you how to install and use popular libraries like **requests**, **NumPy**, and **Pandas** to add more functionality to your programs.
- **Regular Expressions**: Learn to search, extract, and manipulate text patterns using Python's regular expressions. This is an essential skill for data extraction and text processing.
- **Graphical User Interfaces (GUI) with Tkinter**: Take your Python programs to the next level by adding a graphical interface. You'll learn how to create

windows, buttons, and input fields using Tkinter, making your applications more user-friendly.
- **Game Development**: In the capstone project, we'll build a fun and interactive quiz game. This project will help you apply all the concepts you've learned, from functions and control flow to OOP and error handling.

Each chapter is accompanied by a practical project, and all the code used throughout the book can be found on the **official GitHub repository**. The repository contains:

- **Source code** for each project covered in the book.
- **Additional resources** and exercises to help reinforce your learning.

Visit the GitHub repository here:
https://github.com/brewmanandi/learnprogramming.tips-books

But that's not all! If you're hungry for more programming knowledge or curious about the latest in programming education, I highly recommend checking out my site LearnProgramming.tips. It's the go-to resource for discovering everything about learning programming—from tutorials and courses to tips and tricks from expert developers. Keep this website in your bookmarks as you continue your programming journey.

Whether you're building a weather app, developing a to-do list, or crafting a quiz game, this book offers everything you need to master Python through practical, project-based learning. Let's get started!

Chapter 1: Introduction to Python Programming

Overview: Welcome to Python and the Project-Based Approach

Python has quickly become one of the most popular programming languages in the world, and for good reason! Its simplicity, readability, and versatility make it an ideal language for beginners, while still being powerful enough for seasoned developers to build complex applications. From web development to data science, automation, and artificial intelligence, Python is everywhere.

In this book, we'll take a **project-based approach** to learning Python. This means you'll be coding real-world projects from the very start. Each project is designed to teach you a specific set of skills that will build your knowledge incrementally. By the end of this chapter, you'll not only understand the basics of Python programming but also write your first project—a **simple command-line calculator**.

1.1 Why Python?

Before diving into coding, let's take a moment to understand why Python is such a great choice for beginners:

- **Easy to Learn and Read:** Python uses a syntax similar to English, which makes it intuitive. It's often referred to as a "high-level" language, meaning it's designed to be easy for humans to read and write.
- **Versatile:** You can use Python for virtually any kind of programming, from web development and scripting to machine learning and game development.
- **Huge Community and Support:** Python has a massive community of developers, so you'll never struggle to find resources or help when you need it. Additionally, Python's extensive library ecosystem (pre-built code for various tasks) makes your job as a developer much easier.

1.2 Setting Up Python

Installing Python

To begin coding in Python, you'll need to have Python installed on your computer. Fortunately, Python is free and easy to install.

1. **Windows:**
    - Visit the official Python website: https://www.python.org/downloads/

- Click the download button, which will automatically detect your operating system.
- Run the downloaded installer.
- **Important:** During installation, make sure to check the box that says "Add Python to PATH." This ensures you can run Python from any directory on your system.

2. **macOS:**
   - macOS comes with Python pre-installed, but it might not be the latest version.
   - Follow the same instructions as Windows to download and install the latest version of Python.

3. **Linux:**

Most Linux distributions come with Python pre-installed. You can check by opening your terminal and typing:

```
python3 --version
```

If Python is not installed, you can install it by running:

```
sudo apt-get install python3
```

Setting Up a Text Editor

While you can write Python code in any text editor, using a specialized Integrated Development Environment (IDE) will make your life easier.

- **Visual Studio Code (VSCode)**: A free and popular text editor with Python support.
  - Download and install it from https://code.visualstudio.com/.
  - After installation, open VSCode and install the Python extension (search for it in the Extensions tab).

1.3 Running Python Code

Once Python is installed, you can write and run your first Python program.

Using the Command Line:

1. Open a terminal (or command prompt on Windows).
2. Type `python3` (or `python` if on Windows) to enter the Python interactive shell.

Type the following:

```
print("Hello, World!")
```

You should see the output:

```
print("Hello, World!")
```

Using a Python File:

1. Open your text editor (VSCode, for example).
2. Create a new file and save it with the `.py` extension (e.g., `hello.py`)
3. In the file, type:

```
print("Hello, World!")
```

4. Save the file.
5. Go back to the terminal and navigate to the directory where you saved your file.
6. Run the Python file by typing:

```
python3 hello.py
```

You should see the same output:

```
Hello, World!
```

1.4 Understanding Errors and Debugging

As you write code, you will inevitably make mistakes. These mistakes will result in **errors**, also called **exceptions**. When Python encounters an error in your code, it will print an error message to help you understand what went wrong.

Let's see an example of an error:

```
print("Hello, World!"
```

Notice the missing closing parenthesis. When you run this code, Python will display an error message:

```
SyntaxError: unexpected EOF while parsing
```

The error message provides clues about what's wrong. In this case, Python is telling you that there's a problem with the syntax (the structure of the code). **Syntax errors** are the most common errors for beginners.

Debugging Tips:

1. **Read the error message carefully.** Python's error messages are descriptive and usually tell you what's wrong.
2. **Check your syntax.** Are you missing punctuation, like parentheses or colons?
3. **Use print statements.** If you're not sure what's going wrong in a larger program, add `print()` statements to track the values of variables and see what the code is doing at each step.

1.5 Your First Python Project: A Simple Command-Line Calculator

Now that you have a basic understanding of how to write and run Python code, let's jump into your first project—a simple calculator that performs basic arithmetic operations (addition, subtraction, multiplication, and division).

Project Overview:

- The calculator will prompt the user to enter two numbers.
- It will ask the user to choose an operation (addition, subtraction, multiplication, or division).
- It will display the result of the calculation.

Step-by-Step Code:

1. **Get User Input:** Use the `input()` function to ask the user for two numbers and the operation they want to perform.

```python
# Get two numbers from the user
num1 = float(input("Enter the first number: "))
num2 = float(input("Enter the second number: "))

# Ask the user for the operation
operation = input("Enter operation (+, -, *, /): ")
```

2. **Perform the Calculation:** Use `if` statements to decide which operation to perform based on the user's input.

```python
# Perform the calculation
if operation == "+":
    result = num1 + num2
elif operation == "-":
    result = num1 - num2
elif operation == "*":
    result = num1 * num2
elif operation == "/":
    result = num1 / num2
```

```
else:
    result = "Invalid operation"
```

3. **Display the Result:** Finally, print the result of the calculation.

```
# Display the result
print("The result is:", result)
```

Final Code:

```
# Simple command-line calculator

# Get two numbers from the user
num1 = float(input("Enter the first number: "))
num2 = float(input("Enter the second number: "))

# Ask the user for the operation
operation = input("Enter operation (+, -, *, /): ")

# Perform the calculation
if operation == "+":
    result = num1 + num2
elif operation == "-":
    result = num1 - num2
elif operation == "*":
    result = num1 * num2
elif operation == "/":
    result = num1 / num2
else:
    result = "Invalid operation"

# Display the result
print("The result is:", result)
```

Explanation:

- We use input() to get user input, converting the input to a float to handle decimal numbers.
- We use conditional statements (if, elif, else) to decide which operation to perform.
- Finally, the result is displayed using print().

1.6 What You Learned

In this chapter, you learned how to:

- Install and set up Python on your machine.
- Write and run Python code.
- Understand and fix errors.
- Create a simple Python program—a command-line calculator.

Next, we'll dive deeper into Python's core concepts, starting with **variables, data types, and operators** in Chapter 2!

Chapter 2: Variables, Data Types, and Operations

Overview: Understanding the Core Building Blocks of Python

Now that you have written your first Python program, it's time to take a deeper dive into some of the core building blocks of the language: **variables**, **data types**, and **operations**. These concepts form the foundation for writing more complex programs, and by the end of this chapter, you will have a solid understanding of how Python handles data.

In this chapter, you'll learn:

- How to store and manipulate data using variables.
- The various data types available in Python.
- Basic operations such as addition, subtraction, and working with strings.
- How to build your second Python project: a **Temperature Converter**.

2.1 Variables and Assignment

Variables are one of the most basic concepts in programming. Think of them as containers that store information, like numbers or text, which can be used and manipulated later in your program.

Declaring a Variable

In Python, declaring a variable is as simple as assigning a value to it. Here's an example:

```python
name = "Alice"       # String
age = 25             # Integer
temperature = 36.6   # Float
```

In this example:

- `name` is a variable that stores the string `"Alice"`.
- `age` stores the integer `25`.
- `temperature` stores the floating-point number `36.6`.

Python automatically determines the type of data you assign to the variable, so you don't need to specify it.

Reassigning a Variable

You can change the value of a variable at any time by assigning a new value to it:

```python
name = "Bob"
```

Now, `name` stores the string `"Bob"` instead of `"Alice"`.

Variable Naming Rules

- Variable names must start with a letter or an underscore (_).
- They can contain letters, numbers, and underscores, but no spaces.
- They are case-sensitive, meaning `name` and `Name` are two different variables.

Best Practices for Naming Variables

- Use meaningful names: Instead of `x` or `y`, use names that describe the data the variable holds, like `age`, `temperature`, or `user_name`.
- Use snake_case: In Python, the common convention is to use underscores to separate words in variable names (e.g., `user_name`, `first_name`).

2.2 Data Types in Python

Python has several built-in data types that allow you to work with different kinds of data. The most common types you'll encounter as a beginner are:

- **Strings**: Text data.
- **Integers**: Whole numbers.
- **Floats**: Numbers with decimals.
- **Booleans**: True/False values.

Strings

A string is a sequence of characters enclosed in either single (`'`) or double quotes (`"`). Strings are used to represent text.

```python
greeting = "Hello, World!"
```

You can combine strings using **concatenation**:

```python
first_name = "Alice"
last_name = "Smith"
full_name = first_name + " " + last_name
print(full_name)  # Output: Alice Smith
```

Python also provides many built-in string methods, such as:

```python
message = "python programming"
print(message.upper())   # Output: PYTHON PROGRAMMING
print(message.capitalize())   # Output: Python programming
```

Integers and Floats

- **Integers**: Whole numbers, like `5`, `-10`, or `100`.

- **Floats**: Numbers with decimal points, like 3.14 or 0.5.

```
x = 5        # Integer
y = 3.14     # Float
```

Booleans

Booleans represent one of two values: True or False. They are often used in decision-making processes (like in conditional statements).

```
is_sunny = True
is_raining = False
```

2.3 Basic Operations in Python

Now that you know how to store and manage data in variables, let's explore how to manipulate that data using **basic operations**.

Arithmetic Operators

Python supports all basic arithmetic operations:

Addition (+): Adds two numbers.
```
result = 10 + 5   # Output: 15
```

Subtraction (-): Subtracts the second number from the first.
```
result = 10 - 5   # Output: 5
```

Multiplication (*): Multiplies two numbers.
```
result = 10 * 5   # Output: 50
```

Division (/): Divides the first number by the second.
```
result = 10 / 5   # Output: 2.0
```

Integer Division (//): Divides and returns the integer quotient.
```
result = 10 // 3  # Output: 3
```

Modulus (%): Returns the remainder of the division.
```
result = 10 % 3   # Output: 1
```

Exponentiation (**): Raises the first number to the power of the second.
```
result = 2 ** 3   # Output: 8
```

Working with Strings

You can also perform certain operations with strings:

Concatenation (+): Combines two strings.
```
greeting = "Hello" + " " + "World"   # Output: Hello World
```
Repetition (*): Repeats a string a given number of times.
```
laugh = "Ha" * 3   # Output: HaHaHa
```

Casting Between Data Types

Sometimes you need to convert data from one type to another, such as turning a string into an integer or a float. This is called **type casting**.

```
age = "25"
age_as_integer = int(age)   # Converts the string "25" to the integer 25

pi = "3.14"
pi_as_float = float(pi)   # Converts the string "3.14" to the float 3.14
```

You can also cast numbers to strings:

```
number = 100
number_as_string = str(number)   # Converts the integer 100 to the string
"100"
```

Using f-Strings for String Formatting

To make it easier to combine variables with strings, Python provides **f-strings** (formatted string literals). With f-strings, you can insert the value of variables directly into your strings.

```
name = "Alice"
age = 25
message = f"My name is {name} and I am {age} years old."
print(message)   # Output: My name is Alice and I am 25 years old.
```

2.4 Your Second Python Project: Temperature Converter

Now that you understand variables, data types, and basic operations, let's apply this knowledge by building a simple **temperature converter** that converts temperatures between Celsius and Fahrenheit.

Project Overview:

- The program will prompt the user to enter a temperature in either Celsius or Fahrenheit.
- It will convert the temperature to the opposite unit and display the result.

Step-by-Step Code:

1. **Get User Input:** First, we'll ask the user for the temperature and the unit they want to convert from.

```python
temperature = float(input("Enter the temperature: "))
unit = input("Is this in Celsius or Fahrenheit? (C/F): ").upper()
```

2. **Perform the Conversion:** Use conditional statements to check whether the temperature is in Celsius or Fahrenheit, and then convert it accordingly.

```python
if unit == "C":
    # Convert Celsius to Fahrenheit
    converted_temp = (temperature * 9/5) + 32
    print(f"{temperature}°C is equal to {converted_temp}°F")
elif unit == "F":
    # Convert Fahrenheit to Celsius
    converted_temp = (temperature - 32) * 5/9
    print(f"{temperature}°F is equal to {converted_temp}°C")
else:
    print("Invalid input! Please enter 'C' for Celsius or 'F' for Fahrenheit.")
```

Final Code:

```python
# Temperature Converter

# Step 1: Get user input
temperature = float(input("Enter the temperature: "))
unit = input("Is this in Celsius or Fahrenheit? (C/F): ").upper()

# Step 2: Perform the conversion
if unit == "C":
    # Convert Celsius to Fahrenheit
    converted_temp = (temperature * 9/5) + 32
    print(f"{temperature}°C is equal to {converted_temp}°F")
```

```python
elif unit == "F":
    # Convert Fahrenheit to Celsius
    converted_temp = (temperature - 32) * 5/9
    print(f"{temperature}°F is equal to {converted_temp}°C")
else:
    print("Invalid input! Please enter 'C' for Celsius or 'F' for Fahrenheit.")
```

Explanation:

- The program takes input from the user for both the temperature and the unit of measurement.
- It checks whether the input is in Celsius or Fahrenheit and performs the correct conversion using basic arithmetic.
- If the user enters an invalid unit, the program displays an error message.

Example Usage:

```
Enter the temperature: 25
Is this in Celsius or Fahrenheit? (C/F): C
25.0°C is equal to 77.0°F
```

2.5 What You Learned

In this chapter, you learned how to:

- Use variables to store data in Python.
- Work with basic data types like strings, integers, floats, and booleans.
- Perform basic arithmetic operations and manipulate strings.
- Convert data between different types using casting.
- Build a simple temperature converter to apply what you've learned.

Next, in Chapter 3, we'll explore how to make decisions in your programs using **conditional statements and loops**!

This concludes Chapter 2. You've now gained a solid understanding of variables, data types, and operations, and you've built your second Python project!

Chapter 3: Control Flow and Loops

Overview: Writing Programs that Make Decisions

In this chapter, we'll dive into the concept of **control flow**, which enables you to write programs that make decisions and perform actions repeatedly. You'll learn how to use **conditional statements** to execute code based on certain conditions, and how to use **loops** to repeat actions multiple times.

By the end of this chapter, you'll build an interactive game called the **Number Guessing Game** where users will try to guess a randomly generated number, reinforcing the use of both control flow and loops.

3.1 Conditional Statements

What Are Conditional Statements?

Conditional statements allow your program to take different actions based on different conditions. The most common form of conditional statement in Python is the `if` statement, which checks whether a condition is true or false and executes certain code accordingly.

The `if` Statement

Let's start with a simple `if` statement. The syntax looks like this:

```
if condition:
    # code to execute if condition is true
```

Here's an example:

```
age = 18

if age >= 18:
    print("You are an adult.")
```

In this example, Python checks whether the value of `age` is greater than or equal to 18. Since the condition is true, it prints "You are an adult."

The `if-else` Statement

Sometimes you want to execute one block of code if a condition is true, and another block if it's false. You can use an `if-else` statement for this:

```
age = 16

if age >= 18:
    print("You are an adult.")
else:
    print("You are not an adult.")
```

In this case, since age is less than 18, the program will print "You are not an adult."

The `if-elif-else` Statement

For more complex decision-making, you can use multiple conditions with the `elif` (else-if) statement:

```
age = 20

if age < 13:
    print("You are a child.")
elif age < 18:
    print("You are a teenager.")
else:
    print("You are an adult.")
```

In this example:

- If the age is less than 13, the program will print "You are a child."
- If the age is between 13 and 17, it prints "You are a teenager."
- If neither of those conditions is true (the person is 18 or older), it prints "You are an adult."

Comparison Operators

Conditional statements rely on **comparison operators** to compare values. Here are the most common ones:

Operator	Description	Example
==	Equal to	x == y
!=	Not equal to	x != y
>	Greater than	x > y

<	Less than	x < y
>=	Greater than or equal to	x >= y
<=	Less than or equal to	x <= y

For example, you can use the == operator to check if two values are equal:

```
x = 10
if x == 10:
    print("x is 10")
```

Logical Operators

Sometimes, you need to check multiple conditions simultaneously. In Python, you can use **logical operators** like and, or, and not:

- **and**: True only if both conditions are true.
- **or**: True if at least one condition is true.
- **not**: Inverts the value of the condition.

```
age = 20
has_permission = True

if age >= 18 and has_permission:
    print("You are allowed to enter.")
```

3.2 Loops

What Are Loops?

Loops allow your program to execute a block of code repeatedly. Python supports two main types of loops: **for loops** and **while loops**.

The for Loop

A for loop is used when you know in advance how many times you want to repeat a block of code. In Python, for loops are often used to iterate over a sequence like a list or a range of numbers.

The syntax of a for loop looks like this:

```
for variable in sequence:
    # code to execute in each iteration
```

Here's an example that prints the numbers from 1 to 5:

```
for i in range(1, 6):
    print(i)
```

The `range()` function generates a sequence of numbers, and the `for` loop iterates over that sequence. In this case, it prints:

```
1
2
3
4
5
```

The `while` Loop

A `while` loop is used when you want to repeat a block of code as long as a condition is true. The syntax looks like this:

```
while condition:
    # code to execute as long as the condition is true
```

Here's an example of a `while` loop that prints numbers from 1 to 5:

```
i = 1
while i <= 5:
    print(i)
    i += 1    # Increment i by 1
```

In this case, the loop continues to run as long as `i` is less than or equal to 5.

The `break` and `continue` Statements
- `break`: Exits the loop early, regardless of the condition.

```
for i in range(1, 11):
    if i == 5:
        break
    print(i)
```

This prints numbers from 1 to 4 and stops the loop when `i` equals 5.

- `continue`: Skips the rest of the current loop iteration and moves on to the next iteration.

```
for i in range(1, 6):
    if i == 3:
        continue
    print(i)
```

This prints numbers from 1 to 5 but skips 3.

3.3 Your Third Python Project: Number Guessing Game

Now that you have a solid understanding of conditionals and loops, let's put that knowledge to use by building a **Number Guessing Game**. In this game, the computer will randomly select a number, and the user will have to guess what it is. The program will give hints (whether the guess is too high or too low) until the user guesses correctly.

Project Overview:

- The program will generate a random number between 1 and 100.
- The user will be prompted to guess the number.
- After each guess, the program will tell the user whether the guess is too high, too low, or correct.
- The game will continue until the user guesses the correct number.

Step-by-Step Code:

1. **Import the `random` module**:
   We need to generate a random number, so we'll import Python's built-in `random` module.

```
import random
```

2. **Generate a Random Number**:
   The program will randomly select a number between 1 and 100.

```
number_to_guess = random.randint(1, 100)
```

3. **User Input and Guess Evaluation**:
   We'll use a `while` loop to repeatedly ask the user for their guess and give feedback on whether the guess is too high or too low.

```python
# Step 1: Import the random module
import random

# Step 2: Generate a random number between 1 and 100
number_to_guess = random.randint(1, 100)

# Step 3: Initialize a variable to track the number of guesses
guess_count = 0

# Step 4: Loop until the user guesses correctly
while True:
    guess = int(input("Guess a number between 1 and 100: "))
    guess_count += 1

    if guess < number_to_guess:
        print("Too low!")
    elif guess > number_to_guess:
        print("Too high!")
    else:
        print(f"Congratulations! You guessed the number in {guess_count} tries.")
        break
```

Explanation:

- **Step 1:** We import the `random` module to generate a random number.
- **Step 2:** We use `random.randint(1, 100)` to generate a random number between 1 and 100.
- **Step 3:** We initialize a `guess_count` variable to track how many guesses the user makes.
- **Step 4:** A `while` loop keeps asking the user for their guess. Based on the guess, it provides feedback: if the guess is too low, too high, or correct. When the correct number is guessed, the loop ends using the `break` statement.

Final Code:

```python
# Number Guessing Game

import random

# Step 2: Generate a random number between 1 and 100
number_to_guess = random.randint(1, 100)

# Step 3: Initialize a variable to track the number of guesses
```

```
guess_count = 0

# Step 4: Loop until the user guesses correctly
while True:
    guess = int(input("Guess a number between 1 and 100: "))
```

Chapter 4: Functions and Modular Code

Overview: Organizing Code for Reusability and Simplicity

As you progress in programming, you'll find yourself writing code that performs the same task multiple times. Instead of duplicating this code, you can use **functions** to organize your code into reusable blocks. Functions allow you to break your program down into smaller, more manageable pieces. In this chapter, you will learn how to define and call functions, use parameters and return values, and write modular code. By the end of this chapter, you will build a **To-Do List Manager** using functions to structure your code more effectively.

4.1 What Are Functions?

A **function** is a block of code that performs a specific task. Functions allow you to group code that you want to reuse or keep separate for better readability and maintainability.

The Benefits of Functions

- **Code Reusability:** Write once, use many times.
- **Modularity:** Break down large programs into smaller, manageable pieces.
- **Clarity:** Make code more readable and easier to understand.

Function Syntax

To define a function in Python, you use the `def` keyword followed by the function name, parentheses, and a colon. The code inside the function is indented, just like with loops and conditional statements.

```
def greet():
    print("Hello, world!")
```

Once defined, you can call the function by writing its name followed by parentheses:

```
greet()   # Output: Hello, world!
```

4.2 Parameters and Arguments

Sometimes, functions need additional information to do their job. This is where **parameters** and **arguments** come into play.

- **Parameters** are variables listed inside the parentheses in the function definition.
- **Arguments** are the actual values you pass into the function when you call it.

Example:

```
def greet(name):    # 'name' is a parameter
    print(f"Hello, {name}!")

greet("Alice")    # Output: Hello, Alice! ('Alice' is an argument)
greet("Bob")      # Output: Hello, Bob!
```

In this example, the function `greet` takes one parameter (`name`) and prints a personalized greeting.

4.3 Return Values

Functions can also **return** a value to the caller, which allows the function to produce output that can be used elsewhere in the program. To return a value, use the `return` keyword.

Example:

```
def add(a, b):
    return a + b

result = add(5, 3)    # Output: 8
print(result)
```

In this case, the function `add` takes two parameters (`a` and `b`), adds them together, and returns the result. The result is then stored in the variable `result` and printed.

4.4 Default and Keyword Arguments

Functions in Python can have **default parameters**, which allow you to call a function without providing all arguments. The default values are used if no argument is provided for that parameter.

Example:

```
def greet(name="Stranger"):
    print(f"Hello, {name}!")

greet("Alice")    # Output: Hello, Alice!
```

```
greet()              # Output: Hello, Stranger!
```

In this example, the function `greet` has a default parameter value of `"Stranger"`. If no argument is provided when calling the function, it uses the default value.

You can also use **keyword arguments** to explicitly assign values to specific parameters:

```
def introduce(first_name, last_name):
    print(f"Hello, my name is {first_name} {last_name}.")

introduce(first_name="John", last_name="Doe")   # Output: Hello, my name is John Doe.
introduce(last_name="Smith", first_name="Jane") # Output: Hello, my name is Jane Smith.
```

4.5 Scope: Local vs. Global Variables

Variables in Python have **scope**, which determines where they can be accessed within the program. There are two types of scope:

- **Local scope**: Variables defined inside a function are local to that function and cannot be accessed outside of it.
- **Global scope**: Variables defined outside of any function are global and can be accessed anywhere in the program.

Example of Local and Global Scope:

```
# Global variable
greeting = "Hello"

def greet():
    # Local variable
    name = "Alice"
    print(f"{greeting}, {name}!")  # Can access 'greeting' (global) but not 'name' outside this function

greet()  # Output: Hello, Alice!
print(greeting)  # Output: Hello
# print(name)  # This will cause an error, because 'name' is local to the greet() function
```

4.6 Building a To-Do List Manager

Now, let's apply what you've learned by creating a **To-Do List Manager**. This simple program will allow users to add, view, and remove tasks from their to-do list. We'll use functions to break the program into smaller, manageable pieces.

Project Overview:

- Users will be able to:
    - Add a task to the to-do list.
    - View all tasks in the list.
    - Remove a task by its index.
    - Exit the program.

Step-by-Step Code:

1. **Define the Main Menu:** The main menu will prompt users to choose an action.

```python
def show_menu():
    print("\nTo-Do List Manager")
    print("1. Add a task")
    print("2. View tasks")
    print("3. Remove a task")
    print("4. Exit")
```

2. **Create Functions for Each Task:**
- **Add a Task:** This function adds a new task to the list.

```python
def add_task(tasks):
    task = input("Enter a new task: ")
    tasks.append(task)
    print(f"Task '{task}' added.")
```

- **View All Tasks:** This function displays all the tasks in the list.

```python
def view_tasks(tasks):
    if len(tasks) == 0:
        print("Your to-do list is empty!")
    else:
        print("\nYour Tasks:")
        for i, task in enumerate(tasks, start=1):
            print(f"{i}. {task}")
```

- **Remove a Task:** This function removes a task by its index.

```python
def remove_task(tasks):
    view_tasks(tasks)
    if len(tasks) == 0:
        return
    try:
        task_index = int(input("Enter the task number to remove: ")) - 1
        if 0 <= task_index < len(tasks):
            removed_task = tasks.pop(task_index)
            print(f"Task '{removed_task}' removed.")
        else:
            print("Invalid task number!")
    except ValueError:
        print("Please enter a valid number.")
```

3. **Combine Everything in the Main Program Loop:**

```python
def to_do_list_manager():
    tasks = []  # Initialize an empty list for tasks
    while True:
        show_menu()
        choice = input("Choose an option (1-4): ")

        if choice == "1":
            add_task(tasks)
        elif choice == "2":
            view_tasks(tasks)
        elif choice == "3":
            remove_task(tasks)
        elif choice == "4":
            print("Goodbye!")
            break
        else:
            print("Invalid choice, please try again.")

# Run the to-do list manager
to_do_list_manager()
```

Final Code: To-Do List Manager

Here's the full code for your **To-Do List Manager**:

```python
def show_menu():
    print("\nTo-Do List Manager")
    print("1. Add a task")
    print("2. View tasks")
    print("3. Remove a task")
    print("4. Exit")

def add_task(tasks):
    task = input("Enter a new task: ")
    tasks.append(task)
    print(f"Task '{task}' added.")

def view_tasks(tasks):
    if len(tasks) == 0:
        print("Your to-do list is empty!")
    else:
        print("\nYour Tasks:")
        for i, task in enumerate(tasks, start=1):
            print(f"{i}. {task}")

def remove_task(tasks):
    view_tasks(tasks)
    if len(tasks) == 0:
        return
    try:
        task_index = int(input("Enter the task number to remove: ")) - 1
        if 0 <= task_index < len(tasks):
            removed_task = tasks.pop(task_index)
            print(f"Task '{removed_task}' removed.")
        else:
            print("Invalid task number!")
    except ValueError:
        print("Please enter a valid number.")

def to_do_list_manager():
    tasks = []  # Initialize an empty list for tasks
    while True:
        show_menu()
        choice = input("Choose an option (1-4): ")

        if choice == "1":
```

```
            add_task(tasks)
        elif choice == "2":
            view_tasks(tasks)
        elif choice == "3":
            remove_task(tasks)
        elif choice == "4":
            print("Goodbye!")
            break
        else:
            print("Invalid choice, please try again.")

# Run the to-do list manager
to_do_list_manager()
```

4.7 What You Learned

In this chapter, you learned how to:

- Define and call functions in Python.
- Use parameters and return values to make your functions more flexible.
- Organize your code using modular design with functions.
- Write a simple but functional To-Do List Manager using functions.

In the next chapter, we'll explore **lists, tuples, and dictionaries** in Python, which will help you store and manage collections of data more efficiently!

This concludes **Chapter 4** on functions. You're now equipped to write more modular, reusable code with functions, an essential skill for any Python programmer.

Chapter 5: Working with Lists, Tuples, and Dictionaries

Overview: Managing Collections of Data

In this chapter, we're going to explore some of the most essential data structures in Python: **lists**, **tuples**, and **dictionaries**. These structures allow you to manage collections of data efficiently. By the end of this chapter, you'll be building a **Student Grade Tracker**, which will help you practice using lists, tuples, and dictionaries to store, retrieve, and manipulate information.

5.1 Lists: Your Go-To for Ordered Collections

A **list** is a data structure that allows you to store an **ordered collection** of items. Lists are very flexible—you can add, remove, or modify items at any time.

Creating a List

To create a list, simply place items inside square brackets [ ], separated by commas:

```python
fruits = ["apple", "banana", "cherry"]
```

Accessing List Items

List items are accessed using their **index**. Python uses **zero-based indexing**, so the first item has an index of 0:

```python
print(fruits[0])    # Output: apple
print(fruits[2])    # Output: cherry
```

Modifying Lists

You can change the value of a list item by assigning a new value to a specific index:

```python
fruits[1] = "blueberry"
print(fruits)    # Output: ['apple', 'blueberry', 'cherry']
```

You can also add or remove items:

- **Adding an item**: Use the `append()` method to add a new item to the end of the list:

```
fruits.append("orange")
print(fruits)  # Output: ['apple', 'blueberry', 'cherry', 'orange']
```

- **Removing an item**: Use `remove()` to delete an item by its value or `pop()` to remove an item by its index:

```
fruits.remove("blueberry")
print(fruits)  # Output: ['apple', 'cherry', 'orange']
```

Iterating Through a List

You can loop through a list using a `for` loop:

```
for fruit in fruits:
    print(fruit)
```

This will print each item in the list.

5.2 Tuples: Immutable Collections

A **tuple** is similar to a list, but with one key difference: **tuples are immutable**, meaning that once you create a tuple, you cannot change, add, or remove items.

Creating a Tuple

Tuples are created using parentheses `()` instead of square brackets:

```
coordinates = (10.5, 20.3)
```

Accessing Tuple Items

Just like lists, you can access tuple items using their index:

```
print(coordinates[0])  # Output: 10.5
```

Why Use Tuples?

Tuples are useful when you want to create a collection of items that should not change throughout the program. They are also slightly faster than lists in terms of performance, so you might use them when working with constant data.

5.3 Dictionaries: Key-Value Pairs

A **dictionary** is a collection of **key-value pairs**. Unlike lists and tuples that are indexed by position, dictionaries are indexed by **keys**, which can be any immutable type (like strings or numbers).

Creating a Dictionary

Dictionaries are created using curly braces {}. Each key is associated with a value, separated by a colon ::

```
student = {
    "name": "Alice",
    "age": 21,
    "major": "Computer Science"
}
```

Accessing Dictionary Values

You access dictionary values by using their keys:

```
print(student["name"])   # Output: Alice
print(student["age"])    # Output: 21
```

Modifying Dictionaries

You can easily update or add new key-value pairs:

- **Update a value**:

```
student["age"] = 22
print(student)  # Output: {'name': 'Alice', 'age': 22, 'major': 'Computer Science'}
```

- **Add a new key-value pair**:

```
student["graduation_year"] = 2023
print(student)  # Output: {'name': 'Alice', 'age': 22, 'major': 'Computer Science', 'graduation_year': 2023}
```

- **Removing a Key-Value Pair**

You can remove a key-value pair using the `del` statement or the `pop()` method:

```
del student["major"]
print(student)  # Output: {'name': 'Alice', 'age': 22,
'graduation_year': 2023}
```

Iterating Through a Dictionary

You can loop through the keys or values in a dictionary:

```
# Loop through keys
for key in student:
    print(key)

# Loop through values
for value in student.values():
    print(value)

# Loop through both keys and values
for key, value in student.items():
    print(f"{key}: {value}")
```

5.4 Building a Student Grade Tracker

Let's put everything you've learned into practice by creating a **Student Grade Tracker**. In this project, we'll use a dictionary to store student names as keys and their corresponding grades as values.

Project: Student Grade Tracker

Overview:

- The program will allow users to:
    1. Add a student and their grade.
    2. View all students and their grades.
    3. Remove a student by their name.
    4. Exit the program.

Step-by-Step Code:

1. **Define the Main Menu:**

```python
def show_menu():
    print("\n Student Grade Tracker")
    print("1.  Add a student and their grade")
    print("2.  View all students and grades")
    print("3.  Remove a student")
    print("4.  Exit")
```

2. **Function to Add a Student and Grade:**

```python
def add_student(grades):
    name = input("Enter the student's name: ")
    grade = input(f"Enter {name}'s grade: ")
    grades[name] = grade
    print(f"Added {name} with grade '{grade}'. Well done!")
```

3. **Function to View All Students and Grades:**

```python
def view_grades(grades):
    if len(grades) == 0:
        print("No students in the grade tracker. Add some students first!")
    else:
        print("\n Student Grades:")
        for name, grade in grades.items():
            print(f"{name}: {grade}")
```

4. **Function to Remove a Student:**

```python
def remove_student(grades):
    name = input("Enter the student's name to remove: ")
    if name in grades:
        del grades[name]
        print(f"Removed {name} from the tracker.")
    else:
        print(f"Student '{name}' not found.")
```

5. **Main Loop:**

```python
def grade_tracker():
    grades = {}  # Initialize an empty dictionary
    while True:
        show_menu()
```

```python
        choice = input("Choose an option (1-4): ")

        if choice == "1":
            add_student(grades)
        elif choice == "2":
            view_grades(grades)
        elif choice == "3":
            remove_student(grades)
        elif choice == "4":
            print("Goodbye! Hope your students ace their exams!")
            break
        else:
            print("Invalid choice. Please try again.")
```

Final Code: Student Grade Tracker

```python
# Student Grade Tracker

def show_menu():
    print("\n Student Grade Tracker")
    print("1.  Add a student and their grade")
    print("2.  View all students and grades")
    print("3.  Remove a student")
    print("4.  Exit")

def add_student(grades):
    name = input("Enter the student's name: ")
    grade = input(f"Enter {name}'s grade: ")
    grades[name] = grade
    print(f"Added {name} with grade '{grade}'. Well done!")

def view_grades(grades):
    if len(grades) == 0:
        print("No students in the grade tracker. Add some students first!")
    else:
        print("\n Student Grades:")
        for name, grade in grades.items():
            print(f"{name}: {grade}")
```

```python
def remove_student(grades):
    name = input("Enter the student's name to remove: ")
    if name in grades:
        del grades[name]
        print(f"Removed {name} from the tracker.")
    else:
        print(f"Student '{name}' not found.")

def grade_tracker():
    grades = {}  # Initialize an empty dictionary
    while True:
        show_menu()
        choice = input("Choose an option (1-4): ")

        if choice == "1":
            add_student(grades)
        elif choice == "2":
            view_grades(grades)
        elif choice == "3":
            remove_student(grades)
        elif choice == "4":
            print("Goodbye! Hope your students ace their exams!")
            break
        else:
            print("Invalid choice. Please try again.")

# Run the student grade tracker
grade_tracker()
```

5.5 What You Learned

In this chapter, you learned how to:

- Work with lists, tuples, and dictionaries in Python.
- Use lists to manage ordered collections of items.
- Use tuples for immutable collections.
- Use dictionaries to store key-value pairs and access values using keys.
- Build a **Student Grade Tracker** to put these concepts into practice.

In the next chapter, we'll dive into **file handling and data management**, where you'll learn how to read from and write to files to save data persistently.

This concludes **Chapter 5**! Now you're familiar with some of the most important Python data structures, and you've built a handy project to practice using them.

Chapter 6: File Handling and Working with Data

Overview: Storing and Retrieving Data from Files

So far, you've learned how to manipulate data using Python's basic structures such as lists, tuples, and dictionaries. However, all of this data disappears once your program finishes running. In this chapter, we will explore how to **store** and **retrieve data** by working with files. This allows you to make your data persistent—meaning it can be saved for later use.

By the end of this chapter, you'll know how to:

- Read from and write to files.
- Work with text files and CSV files.
- Handle file-related exceptions.
- Build a simple **Contact Book** that stores data in a file.

6.1 Why Work with Files?

In most programs, you want to store data permanently so that it can be used again after the program has been closed. Whether you're saving user preferences, game scores, or a database of contacts, file handling is an essential skill in programming. Python provides several built-in functions and libraries to work with files effectively.

6.2 Working with Text Files

Opening a File

In Python, you can open a file using the `open()` function. This function requires the name of the file and the mode in which you want to open it. The most common modes are:

- **'r'**: Open a file for reading (default).
- **'w'**: Open a file for writing (creates a new file or overwrites an existing one).
- **'a'**: Open a file for appending (adds data to the end of the file without overwriting it).

```python
# Opening a file for reading
file = open("example.txt", "r")
```

```python
# Opening a file for writing
file = open("example.txt", "w")

# Opening a file for appending
file = open("example.txt", "a")
```

Reading from a File

Once a file is opened in read mode, you can use methods like `read()`, `readline()`, or `readlines()` to read its content.

- `read()`: Reads the entire file as a single string.

```python
file = open("example.txt", "r")
content = file.read()
print(content)
file.close()
```

- `readline()`: Reads one line at a time.

```python
file = open("example.txt", "r")
line = file.readline()
print(line)
file.close()
```

- `readlines()`: Reads all lines and returns them as a list of strings.

```python
file = open("example.txt", "r")
lines = file.readlines()
for line in lines:
    print(line.strip())
file.close()
```

Writing to a File

To write data to a file, you can open the file in write mode (`'w'`) or append mode (`'a'`). Be careful with write mode—it will overwrite the file's content if it already exists.

- **Writing to a file**:

```python
file = open("example.txt", "w")
file.write("Hello, this is a test.\n")
```

```
file.write("Writing to a file is easy!\n")
file.close()
```

- **Appending to a file**:

```
file = open("example.txt", "a")
file.write("Appending some more content.\n")
file.close()
```

- **Closing a File**

Whenever you open a file, it's important to close it after you're done working with it. This ensures that all changes are saved and that the file is properly released by the program.

```
file.close()
```

The `with` Statement

Using the `with` statement is the best way to open and close files because it automatically closes the file for you, even if an error occurs.

```
with open("example.txt", "r") as file:
    content = file.read()
    print(content)
# No need to explicitly call file.close() here
```

6.3 Handling Exceptions with Files

Sometimes things go wrong when working with files. The file might not exist, or there could be permission issues. In these cases, Python will raise an exception. You can handle these potential problems using `try-except` blocks.

```
try:
    with open("nonexistentfile.txt", "r") as file:
        content = file.read()
except FileNotFoundError:
    print("The file you are trying to open does not exist.")
```

6.4 Working with CSV Files

CSV (Comma-Separated Values) files are a popular format for storing tabular data. Python provides a built-in `csv` module to handle these types of files.

Reading a CSV File

You can use the `csv.reader` object to read from a CSV file. It reads the file line by line and splits each line into a list of values.

```python
import csv

with open("data.csv", "r") as file:
    reader = csv.reader(file)
    for row in reader:
        print(row)
```

Writing to a CSV File

To write data to a CSV file, you can use the `csv.writer` object:

```python
import csv

with open("data.csv", "w", newline="") as file:
    writer = csv.writer(file)
    writer.writerow(["Name", "Age", "Occupation"])
    writer.writerow(["Alice", 30, "Engineer"])
    writer.writerow(["Bob", 25, "Designer"])
```

6.5 Building a Contact Book

Let's apply everything we've learned so far to create a simple **Contact Book**. This program will store contacts (name, phone number, and email) in a text file. Users will be able to add, view, and search for contacts.

Project: Contact Book

Overview

- The Contact Book program allows users to:
    1. Add a contact (name, phone number, and email) to the contact book.
    2. View all saved contacts.
    3. Search for a contact by name.
    4. Exit the program.

Step-by-Step Code

1. **Define the Main Menu**

```python
def show_menu():
    print("\n Contact Book")
    print("1.  Add a new contact")
    print("2.  View all contacts")
    print("3.  Search for a contact by name")
    print("4.  Exit")
```

2. **Function to Add a Contact**

```python
def add_contact():
    name = input("Enter the contact's name: ")
    phone = input("Enter the contact's phone number: ")
    email = input("Enter the contact's email address: ")

    with open("contacts.txt", "a") as file:
        file.write(f"{name},{phone},{email}\n")

    print(f"Contact {name} has been added.")
```

3. **Function to View All Contacts**

```python
def view_contacts():
    try:
        with open("contacts.txt", "r") as file:
            contacts = file.readlines()

            if len(contacts) == 0:
                print("No contacts found. Start adding some!")
            else:
                print("\n All Contacts:")
                for contact in contacts:
                    name, phone, email = contact.strip().split(",")
                    print(f"Name: {name}, Phone: {phone}, Email: {email}")
    except FileNotFoundError:
        print("No contacts file found. Start by adding a contact!")
```

4. **Function to Search for a Contact**

```python
def search_contact():
    search_name = input("Enter the name of the contact to search for: ").lower()

    try:
        with open("contacts.txt", "r") as file:
            contacts = file.readlines()

            found = False
            for contact in contacts:
                name, phone, email = contact.strip().split(",")
                if search_name == name.lower():
                    print(f"  Found: {name}, Phone: {phone}, Email: {email}")
                    found = True
                    break

            if not found:
                print(f"No contact found with the name {search_name}.")
    except FileNotFoundError:
        print("No contacts file found. Start by adding a contact!")
```

5. **Main Program Loop**

```python
def contact_book():
    while True:
        show_menu()
        choice = input("Choose an option (1-4): ")

        if choice == "1":
            add_contact()
        elif choice == "2":
            view_contacts()
        elif choice == "3":
            search_contact()
        elif choice == "4":
            print("Goodbye! Don't forget to keep in touch with your contacts!  ")
```

```
            break
        else:
            print("Invalid option. Please try again.")
```

Final Code: Contact Book

Here's the full code for the **Contact Book** project:

```python
# Contact Book

def show_menu():
    print("\n Contact Book")
    print("1.  Add a new contact")
    print("2.  View all contacts")
    print("3.  Search for a contact by name")
    print("4.  Exit")

def add_contact():
    name = input("Enter the contact's name: ")
    phone = input("Enter the contact's phone number: ")
    email = input("Enter the contact's email address: ")

    with open("contacts.txt", "a") as file:
        file.write(f"{name},{phone},{email}\\n")

    print(f"Contact {name} has been added.")

def view_contacts():
    try:
        with open("contacts.txt", "r") as file:
            contacts = file.readlines()

            if len(contacts) == 0:
                print("No contacts found. Start adding some!")
            else:
                print("\\n All Contacts:")
                for contact in contacts:
                    name, phone, email = contact.strip().split(",")
                    print(f"Name: {name}, Phone: {phone}, Email: {email}")
```

```python
    except FileNotFoundError:
        print("No contacts file found. Start by adding a contact!")

def search_contact():
    search_name = input("Enter the name of the contact to search for: ").lower()

    try:
        with open("contacts.txt", "r") as file:
            contacts = file.readlines()

            found = False
            for contact in contacts:
                name, phone, email = contact.strip().split(",")
                if search_name == name.lower():
                    print(f"□ Found: {name}, Phone: {phone}, Email: {email}")
                    found = True
                    break

            if not found:
                print(f"No contact found with the name {search_name}.")
    except FileNotFoundError:
        print("No contacts file found. Start by adding a contact!")

def contact_book():
    while True:
        show_menu()
        choice = input("Choose an option (1-4): ")

        if choice == "1":
            add_contact()
        elif choice == "2":
            view_contacts()
        elif choice == "3":
            search_contact()
        elif choice == "4":
            print("Goodbye! Don't forget to keep in touch with your contacts! □")
```

```
            break
        else:
            print("Invalid option. Please try again.")

# Run the Contact Book program
contact_book()
```

6.6 What You Learned

In this chapter, you learned:

- How to work with files to store and retrieve data.
- How to handle text files and CSV files.
- How to read from and write to files in Python.
- How to build a **Contact Book** that uses file handling to save data persistently.

In the next chapter, we'll dive into **object-oriented programming (OOP)**, a powerful paradigm that will allow you to organize your code in a more structured and reusable way!

This concludes **Chapter 6**! You're now equipped with the skills to make your programs save data, which is an essential part of building real-world applications.

Chapter 7: Introduction to Object-Oriented Programming (OOP)

Overview: Understanding Object-Oriented Programming

Object-Oriented Programming (OOP) is one of the most popular and powerful programming paradigms. OOP helps you organize your code by modeling real-world entities as **objects** that have both attributes (data) and behaviors (methods). This approach makes your code more structured, reusable, and easier to maintain.

In this chapter, we'll explore the fundamental concepts of OOP, such as **classes**, **objects**, **attributes**, **methods**, and **inheritance**. By the end of this chapter, you'll build a **Bank Account Management System** that leverages OOP principles to manage different types of accounts.

7.1 What Is Object-Oriented Programming (OOP)?

OOP is based on the idea of organizing your code around **objects**. An object is a self-contained piece of code that contains:

- **Attributes**: These are the properties or data associated with the object.
- **Methods**: These are the actions the object can perform (functions that belong to the object).

Example:

Think of a **car** as an object:

- **Attributes**: Brand, color, speed, etc.
- **Methods**: Drive, stop, honk, etc.

In OOP, you define **classes** to create objects. A class is like a blueprint for objects, and each object created from the class is called an **instance**.

7.2 Classes and Objects

Defining a Class

A **class** is a blueprint for creating objects. You define a class using the `class` keyword. Inside the class, you define the attributes and methods that will belong to the objects created from that class.

```python
class Car:
    # Constructor method to initialize the attributes
    def __init__(self, brand, color):
        self.brand = brand  # Attribute
        self.color = color  # Attribute

    # Method to display car details
    def display_info(self):
        print(f"This car is a {self.color} {self.brand}.")
```

In the example above, the `Car` class has two attributes: `brand` and `color`. It also has one method, `display_info()`, that prints out the car's details.

Creating an Object (Instance)

Once the class is defined, you can create objects (instances) of the class.

```python
# Create an object of the Car class
my_car = Car("Toyota", "red")

# Access attributes and methods
print(my_car.brand)  # Output: Toyota
my_car.display_info()  # Output: This car is a red Toyota.
```

In this case, `my_car` is an object of the class `Car`. It has its own `brand` and `color`, which we can access and modify.

7.3 Attributes and Methods

Attributes (Instance Variables)

Attributes, also known as instance variables, hold data specific to an object. They are defined inside the `__init__()` method, which is the **constructor** of the class. The constructor initializes the object's attributes when it is created.

```python
class Dog:
    def __init__(self, name, breed):
        self.name = name  # Attribute
        self.breed = breed  # Attribute

# Create an object of the Dog class
my_dog = Dog("Rex", "German Shepherd")
```

```
print(my_dog.name)  # Output: Rex
```

Methods (Instance Methods)

Methods are functions that belong to an object. They are defined inside the class and typically operate on the object's attributes.

```
class Dog:
    def __init__(self, name, breed):
        self.name = name
        self.breed = breed

    # Method to make the dog bark
    def bark(self):
        print(f"{self.name} says woof!")

my_dog = Dog("Rex", "German Shepherd")
my_dog.bark()  # Output: Rex says woof!
```

7.4 Encapsulation

Encapsulation is the practice of restricting access to certain attributes and methods of an object. This helps protect the internal state of an object and allows for better control over how the data is accessed or modified.

In Python, you can make attributes or methods **private** by prefixing them with a double underscore __.

```
class BankAccount:
    def __init__(self, account_holder, balance):
        self.account_holder = account_holder
        self.__balance = balance  # Private attribute

    def deposit(self, amount):
        if amount > 0:
            self.__balance += amount
            print(f"Deposited {amount}. New balance: {self.__balance}")
        else:
            print("Deposit amount must be positive.")

    def __private_method(self):
```

```
        print("This is a private method.")
```

In the example above, `__balance` is a private attribute, and `__private_method()` is a private method. You cannot access them directly from outside the class.

```
account = BankAccount("Alice", 1000)
account.__balance  # This will raise an error
```

7.5 Inheritance

Inheritance allows one class to inherit attributes and methods from another class. This helps with code reuse and creating hierarchies of related classes.

Parent Class (Base Class)

The class that is being inherited from is called the **parent class** or **base class**.

Child Class (Derived Class)

The class that inherits from the parent class is called the **child class** or **derived class**. It inherits all the attributes and methods of the parent class but can also have its own attributes and methods.

```python
# Parent class
class Animal:
    def __init__(self, name):
        self.name = name

    def make_sound(self):
        print(f"{self.name} makes a sound.")

# Child class (inherits from Animal)
class Dog(Animal):
    def make_sound(self):
        print(f"{self.name} barks!")

# Create an object of the Dog class
my_dog = Dog("Rex")
my_dog.make_sound()  # Output: Rex barks!
```

In this example, the `Dog` class inherits from the `Animal` class and overrides the `make_sound()` method.

7.6 Polymorphism

Polymorphism allows you to use a single method name in different ways for different classes. It's a way to define methods in the child classes that have the same name as methods in the parent class but behave differently.

For example:

```python
class Cat(Animal):
    def make_sound(self):
        print(f"{self.name} meows!")

# Create objects of both Dog and Cat classes
my_dog = Dog("Rex")
my_cat = Cat("Whiskers")

# Both objects have the same method, but it behaves differently
my_dog.make_sound()   # Output: Rex barks!
my_cat.make_sound()   # Output: Whiskers meows!
```

Here, both `Dog` and `Cat` inherit from `Animal` and have a method called `make_sound()`, but the method behaves differently for each class.

7.7 Building a Bank Account Management System

Now that we've covered the basics of OOP, let's build a **Bank Account Management System**. This system will use OOP principles to manage different types of bank accounts, such as savings and checking accounts. You'll be able to:

1. Create new accounts.
2. Deposit money into accounts.
3. Withdraw money from accounts.
4. Display account details.

Project: Bank Account Management System

Overview

We will create a base class called `BankAccount` that holds the common attributes (like account holder and balance) and methods (like deposit and withdraw). We will then create child classes for **CheckingAccount** and **SavingsAccount**, which will inherit from `BankAccount`.

Step-by-Step Code

1. **Define the BankAccount Base Class**

```python
class BankAccount:
    def __init__(self, account_holder, balance=0):
        self.account_holder = account_holder
        self.balance = balance

    def deposit(self, amount):
        if amount > 0:
            self.balance += amount
            print(f"Deposited {amount}. New balance: {self.balance}")
        else:
            print("Deposit amount must be positive.")

    def withdraw(self, amount):
        if amount > self.balance:
            print("Insufficient funds!")
        else:
            self.balance -= amount
            print(f"Withdrew {amount}. New balance: {self.balance}")

    def display_info(self):
        print(f"Account Holder: {self.account_holder}")
        print(f"Balance: {self.balance}")
```

2. **Create a Child Class for Checking Accounts**

```python
class CheckingAccount(BankAccount):
    def __init__(self, account_holder, balance=0):
        super().__init__(account_holder, balance)
        self.overdraft_limit = 500  # Example of an additional attribute

    def withdraw(self, amount):
```

```python
        if amount > self.balance + self.overdraft_limit:
            print("Exceeded overdraft limit!")
        else:
            self.balance -= amount
            print(f"Withdrew {amount}. New balance: {self.balance}")
```

3. **Create a Child Class for Savings Accounts**

```python
class SavingsAccount(BankAccount):
    def __init__(self, account_holder, balance=0):
        super().__init__(account_holder, balance)
        self.interest_rate = 0.02  # Example of an additional attribute

    def add_interest(self):
        interest = self.balance * self.interest_rate
        self.balance += interest
        print(f"Added interest: {interest}. New balance: {self.balance}")
```

4. **Main Program to Test the Bank Account System**

```python
def main():
    # Create a checking account
    checking_account = CheckingAccount("Alice", 1000)
    checking_account.display_info()
    checking_account.withdraw(1200)
    checking_account.deposit(500)

    print("\n")

    # Create a savings account
    savings_account = SavingsAccount("Bob", 2000)
    savings_account.display_info()
    savings_account.add_interest()

if __name__ == "__main__":
    main()
```

Final Code: Bank Account Management System

```python
class BankAccount:
    def __init__(self, account_holder, balance=0):
        self.account_holder = account_holder
        self.balance = balance

    def deposit(self, amount):
        if amount > 0:
            self.balance += amount
            print(f"Deposited {amount}. New balance: {self.balance}")
        else:
            print("Deposit amount must be positive.")

    def withdraw(self, amount):
        if amount > self.balance:
            print("Insufficient funds!")
        else:
            self.balance -= amount
            print(f"Withdrew {amount}. New balance: {self.balance}")

    def display_info(self):
        print(f"Account Holder: {self.account_holder}")
        print(f"Balance: {self.balance}")


class CheckingAccount(BankAccount):
    def __init__(self, account_holder, balance=0):
        super().__init__(account_holder, balance)
        self.overdraft_limit = 500

    def withdraw(self, amount):
        if amount > self.balance + self.overdraft_limit:
            print("Exceeded overdraft limit!")
        else:
            self.balance -= amount
            print(f"Withdrew {amount}. New balance: {self.balance}")


class SavingsAccount(BankAccount):
    def __init__(self, account_holder, balance=0):
```

```python
        super().__init__(account_holder, balance)
        self.interest_rate = 0.02

    def add_interest(self):
        interest = self.balance * self.interest_rate
        self.balance += interest
        print(f"Added interest: {interest}. New balance: {self.balance}")


def main():
    # Create a checking account
    checking_account = CheckingAccount("Alice", 1000)
    checking_account.display_info()
    checking_account.withdraw(1200)
    checking_account.deposit(500)

    print("\n")

    # Create a savings account
    savings_account = SavingsAccount("Bob", 2000)
    savings_account.display_info()
    savings_account.add_interest()


if __name__ == "__main__":
    main()
```

7.8 What You Learned

In this chapter, you learned:

- The core principles of **Object-Oriented Programming (OOP)**.
- How to create and use **classes** and **objects**.
- How to define and access **attributes** and **methods**.
- How to use **inheritance** to create child classes.
- How to apply **polymorphism** to make your methods more flexible.
- Built a **Bank Account Management System** using OOP principles.

In the next chapter, we'll explore **error handling** and how to make your programs more robust by managing exceptions effectively!

This concludes **Chapter 7**! You've taken a big step toward mastering Python by learning the powerful concepts of OOP. Keep practicing getting comfortable with these ideas, as they are widely used in real-world programming.

Chapter 8: Error Handling and Debugging

Overview: Making Your Programs More Robust

When writing code, errors are inevitable. Some errors happen because of mistakes in the code (bugs), and others are caused by external factors, such as invalid user input or missing files. In this chapter, you'll learn how to make your programs more robust by handling errors gracefully. You'll also explore debugging techniques to help you find and fix issues in your code.

By the end of this chapter, you'll be able to:

- Understand different types of errors.
- Use Python's **exception handling** system to deal with errors.
- Apply common debugging techniques to troubleshoot issues.
- Build a **To-Do List Manager with Error Handling** to reinforce your understanding.

8.1 Types of Errors in Python

In Python, errors are categorized into different types:

1. Syntax Errors

- Occur when Python can't interpret your code due to incorrect syntax (grammar mistakes in the code).
- Example:

```
print("Hello, World!
```

Error Message:

```
SyntaxError: EOL while scanning string literal
```

2. Runtime Errors (Exceptions)

- Occur during the execution of your program, causing the program to crash unless handled.
- Example:

```
result = 10 / 0
```

Error Message:

```
ZeroDivisionError: division by zero
```

3. Logical Errors

- Occur when the code runs without errors, but the output is incorrect due to faulty logic.
- Example: A function that is supposed to calculate the area of a rectangle but accidentally returns the perimeter.

8.2 Exception Handling in Python

Python uses a system of **exceptions** to handle runtime errors. An exception is an event that occurs during the execution of a program and disrupts the normal flow of instructions. To prevent the program from crashing, you can use **try-except** blocks to handle exceptions.

Basic Try-Except Block

The **try-except** block lets you catch and handle exceptions gracefully. Here's the basic structure:

```python
try:
    # Code that might raise an exception
    risky_operation()
except SomeException:
    # Code to handle the exception
    print("An error occurred.")
```

Example: Handling Division by Zero

```python
try:
    result = 10 / 0
except ZeroDivisionError:
    print("Oops! You can't divide by zero.")
```

8.3 Catching Multiple Exceptions

You can handle multiple types of exceptions by using multiple `except` blocks. This is useful when different exceptions require different handling.

Example: Handling Multiple Exceptions

```python
try:
    number = int(input("Enter a number: "))
    result = 10 / number
except ValueError:
    print("Please enter a valid number.")
except ZeroDivisionError:
    print("Oops! You can't divide by zero.")
```

In this example, if the user enters a non-numeric value, it raises a `ValueError`. If they enter 0, it raises a `ZeroDivisionError`.

8.4 The `else` and `finally` Clauses

You can use the `else` clause to specify code that should only run if no exceptions are raised. The `finally` clause, on the other hand, will run whether an exception occurred or not. This is useful for cleaning up resources, such as closing files or releasing network connections.

Example: Using `else` and `finally`

```python
try:
    number = int(input("Enter a number: "))
    result = 10 / number
except ZeroDivisionError:
    print("Oops! You can't divide by zero.")
else:
    print(f"Result: {result}")
finally:
    print("End of program.")
```

In this example:

- If no exception occurs, the result is printed, followed by "End of program."
- If an exception occurs, the error message is printed, but the `finally` block will still run.

8.5 Raising Your Own Exceptions

In addition to catching exceptions, you can also **raise exceptions** when certain conditions are met in your code. This can help you enforce specific rules or validations.

Example: Raising an Exception

```python
def withdraw_money(amount, balance):
    if amount > balance:
        raise ValueError("Insufficient funds!")
    else:
        balance -= amount
        print(f"Withdrew {amount}. New balance: {balance}")

try:
    withdraw_money(500, 300)
except ValueError as e:
    print(e)
```

In this example, we manually raise a `ValueError` if the user tries to withdraw more money than they have in their balance.

8.6 Common Exception Types in Python

Here are some common exceptions you might encounter in Python:

`ValueError`: Raised when a function gets an argument of the right type but with an inappropriate value (e.g., trying to convert a string that doesn't represent a number into an integer).

```python
int("Hello")   # ValueError: invalid literal for int() with base 10
```

- `ZeroDivisionError`: Raised when you try to divide by zero.

```python
10 / 0   # ZeroDivisionError: division by zero
```

- `TypeError`: Raised when an operation or function is applied to an object of inappropriate type.

```python
"5" + 5   # TypeError: can only concatenate str (not "int") to str
```

- `FileNotFoundError`: Raised when trying to open a file that doesn't exist.

```python
open("nonexistentfile.txt")   # FileNotFoundError: No such file or directory
```

8.7 Debugging Techniques

Even the best programmers encounter bugs. Debugging is the process of identifying and fixing issues in your code. Let's explore some useful debugging techniques:

1. Print Statements

One of the simplest ways to debug is to use `print()` statements to display the values of variables at different points in your program. This can help you track down where things go wrong.

```python
def add_numbers(a, b):
    print(f"a: {a}, b: {b}")
    return a + b

result = add_numbers(5, "ten")   # Will throw an error
```

The `print()` statement helps you see the values of a and b before the error occurs.

2. Using `assert` for Debugging

The `assert` statement can be used to check conditions in your code. If the condition evaluates to `False`, the program raises an `AssertionError`.

```python
def divide_numbers(a, b):
    assert b != 0, "b cannot be zero"
    return a / b

divide_numbers(10, 0)   # Will raise an AssertionError
```

3. Using a Debugger

Python has a built-in debugger called `pdb`. You can step through your code line by line, examine variables, and see how your program executes in real time. To start debugging, you can import `pdb` and set a breakpoint using `pdb.set_trace()`.

```python
import pdb

def multiply(a, b):
    pdb.set_trace()   # Set a breakpoint here
    return a * b

result = multiply(5, 3)
print(result)
```

When you run the program, it will pause at the breakpoint, and you can inspect the program state and step through it.

8.8 Building a To-Do List Manager with Error Handling

Now, let's apply what you've learned by building a **To-Do List Manager** that includes error handling for invalid inputs, empty task lists, and more.

Project Overview:

- Users will be able to:
    1. Add tasks to the to-do list.
    2. View all tasks.
    3. Remove tasks by their index.
    4. Exit the program.

The program will handle errors like:

- Non-numeric input when removing a task.
- Trying to remove a task from an empty list.

Step-by-Step Code

1. **Define the Main Menu**

```
def show_menu():
    print("\nTo-Do List Manager")
    print("1. Add a task")
    print("2. View tasks")
    print("3. Remove a task")
    print("4. Exit")
```

2. **Function to Add a Task**

```
def add_task(tasks):
    task = input("Enter a new task: ")
    tasks.append(task)
    print(f"Task '{task}' added.")
```

3. **Function to View All Tasks**

```
def view_tasks(tasks):
    if len(tasks) == 0:
```

```python
            print("No tasks in your to-do list.")
    else:
        print("\nYour To-Do List:")
        for i, task in enumerate(tasks, start=1):
            print(f"{i}. {task}")
```

4. **Function to Remove a Task with Error Handling**

```python
def remove_task(tasks):
    view_tasks(tasks)

    if len(tasks) == 0:
        return  # No tasks to remove

    try:
        task_index = int(input("Enter the task number to remove: ")) - 1

        if 0 <= task_index < len(tasks):
            removed_task = tasks.pop(task_index)
            print(f"Task '{removed_task}' removed.")
        else:
            print("Invalid task number.")
    except ValueError:
        print("Please enter a valid number.")
```

5. **Main Program Loop with Error Handling**

```python
def to_do_list_manager():
    tasks = []  # Start with an empty list of tasks
    while True:
        show_menu()
        choice = input("Choose an option (1-4): ")

        if choice == "1":
            add_task(tasks)
        elif choice == "2":
            view_tasks(tasks)
        elif choice == "3":
            remove_task(tasks)
        elif choice == "4":
            print("Goodbye!")
```

```
            break
        else:
            print("Invalid choice. Please enter a number between 1 and 4.")
```

Final Code: To-Do List Manager with Error Handling

Here's the complete code for your **To-Do List Manager**:

```python
def show_menu():
    print("\nTo-Do List Manager")
    print("1. Add a task")
    print("2. View tasks")
    print("3. Remove a task")
    print("4. Exit")


def add_task(tasks):
    task = input("Enter a new task: ")
    tasks.append(task)
    print(f"Task '{task}' added.")

def view_tasks(tasks):
    if len(tasks) == 0:
        print("No tasks in your to-do list.")
    else:
        print("\nYour To-Do List:")
        for i, task in enumerate(tasks, start=1):
            print(f"{i}. {task}")

def remove_task(tasks):
    view_tasks(tasks)

    if len(tasks) == 0:
        return

    try:
        task_index = int(input("Enter the task number to remove: ")) - 1

        if 0 <= task_index < len(tasks):
            removed_task = tasks.pop(task_index)
```

```python
            print(f"Task '{removed_task}' removed.")
        else:
            print("Invalid task number.")
    except ValueError:
        print("Please enter a valid number.")

def to_do_list_manager():
    tasks = []
    while True:
        show_menu()
        choice = input("Choose an option (1-4): ")

        if choice == "1":
            add_task(tasks)
        elif choice == "2":
            view_tasks(tasks)
        elif choice == "3":
            remove_task(tasks)
        elif choice == "4":
            print("Goodbye!")
            break
        else:
            print("Invalid choice. Please enter a number between 1 and 4.")

# Run the to-do list manager
to_do_list_manager()
```

8.9 What You Learned

In this chapter, you learned:

- The different types of errors in Python (syntax, runtime, logical).
- How to use **try-except** blocks to handle exceptions.
- How to raise and catch exceptions.
- Common exception types in Python.
- Useful debugging techniques, including `print()`, `assert`, and using Python's `pdb` debugger.
- How to build a **To-Do List Manager** that incorporates error handling for invalid inputs.

In the next chapter, we'll dive into **working with external libraries** and see how to extend Python's functionality with powerful third-party tools.

This concludes **Chapter 8**! You're now equipped to handle errors in your programs, making them more robust and user-friendly. Keep practicing, becoming proficient in debugging and handling exceptions effectively.

Chapter 9: Working with External Libraries and Modules

Overview: Extending Python's Power

Python's standard library is incredibly rich, offering modules and functions to tackle most common tasks. However, sometimes you need functionality that goes beyond the standard library. This is where **external libraries** and **modules** come in. These libraries offer pre-built code to extend Python's capabilities, allowing you to accomplish complex tasks without reinventing the wheel.

In this chapter, you'll learn:

- How to install and use external libraries.
- The basics of working with popular libraries such as **requests**, **NumPy**, and **Pandas**.
- How to organize and import modules effectively.
- You'll finish by building a **Weather App** that fetches real-time weather data using an external API.

9.1 What Are External Libraries?

External libraries are packages of code that provide additional functionality, beyond what the standard Python library offers. They are created and maintained by the Python community and are usually hosted on the **Python Package Index (PyPI)**, a repository of open-source Python packages.

9.2 Installing External Libraries with pip

Python's package manager, **pip**, allows you to easily install external libraries. Pip is included with Python installations by default. You can use pip to install, upgrade, or uninstall Python packages.

Basic pip Commands

- **Install a package**:

```
pip install package_name
```

- **Upgrade a package**:

```
pip install --upgrade package_name
```

- **Uninstall a package**:

```
pip uninstall package_name
```

- **Example: Installing** `requests` **Library**

The `requests` library is a popular library for making HTTP requests in Python. To install it, use the following command:

```
pip install requests
```

Once installed, you can use the library in your Python code.

```
import requests

response = requests.get("https://api.github.com")
print(response.status_code)   # Output: 200
```

9.3 Popular External Libraries

Let's take a look at three popular external libraries: **requests**, **NumPy**, and **Pandas**. Each of these libraries solves specific problems and extends Python's capabilities in different domains.

1. The `requests` Library

The `requests` library simplifies making HTTP requests. It allows you to interact with web services (APIs), download web pages, and handle HTTP methods (GET, POST, PUT, DELETE).

Basic Example: Making a GET Request

```
import requests

# Fetching data from an API
response = requests.get("https://api.github.com")

# Checking the status code
if response.status_code == 200:
    print("Success!")
```

```
        print(response.json())  # Returns the response data in JSON
format
else:
    print("Failed to retrieve data.")
```

Sending POST Data

You can send data to a web server using a POST request. Here's an example:

```
import requests

data = {"name": "John", "age": 30}
response = requests.post("https://httpbin.org/post", json=data)
print(response.json())  # Returns the server's response as JSON
```

2. The NumPy Library

The NumPy library is widely used for scientific computing. It provides support for arrays, matrices, and a large collection of mathematical functions. If you're working with large datasets or performing numerical computations, NumPy is indispensable.

Installing NumPy

```
pip install numpy
```

Basic Example: Creating a NumPy Array

```
import numpy as np

# Creating a 1D array
array = np.array([1, 2, 3, 4, 5])
print(array)  # Output: [1 2 3 4 5]

# Performing basic operations
print(array + 10)  # Output: [11 12 13 14 15]
print(array * 2)   # Output: [ 2  4  6  8 10]
```

2D Arrays and Matrix Operations

```
# Creating a 2D array (matrix)
matrix = np.array([[1, 2], [3, 4]])
print(matrix)
# Output:
# [[1 2]
```

```
#  [3 4]]

# Transposing the matrix
transpose = matrix.T
print(transpose)
# Output:
# [[1 3]
#  [2 4]]
```

3. The Pandas Library

Pandas is a powerful library for data manipulation and analysis. It introduces two key data structures: **Series** (1D) and **DataFrame** (2D). These data structures make it easy to work with tabular data, like the data you'd find in a spreadsheet.

Installing Pandas

```
pip install pandas
```

Basic Example: Creating a DataFrame

```python
import pandas as pd

# Creating a DataFrame from a dictionary
data = {"Name": ["Alice", "Bob", "Charlie"], "Age": [25, 30, 35]}
df = pd.DataFrame(data)
print(df)
```

Output:

```
      Name  Age
0    Alice   25
1      Bob   30
2  Charlie   35
```

Reading Data from a CSV File

Pandas can read data from various file formats, including CSV. Here's how to read a CSV file into a DataFrame:

```python
df = pd.read_csv("data.csv")
print(df.head())  # Display the first 5 rows of the DataFrame
```

Basic Operations with Pandas

```python
# Filtering data
adults = df[df["Age"] > 18]
print(adults)

# Adding a new column
df["Salary"] = [50000, 60000, 70000]
print(df)

# Descriptive statistics
print(df.describe())  # Outputs basic statistics like mean, std, etc.
```

9.4 Organizing Code with Modules

A **module** is simply a Python file containing functions, classes, and variables that you can use in other Python files. Modules allow you to organize your code into separate files, making it more modular and maintainable.

Creating and Importing a Module

Let's create a module called `math_operations.py` with two simple functions.

```python
# math_operations.py

def add(a, b):
    return a + b

def subtract(a, b):
    return a - b
```

Now, you can import this module into another Python file and use its functions.

```python
# main.py

import math_operations as mo

result = mo.add(5, 3)
print(result)  # Output: 8
```

Importing Specific Functions

You can also import specific functions from a module, like this:

```
from math_operations import add

result = add(10, 5)
print(result)  # Output: 15
```

9.5 Building a Weather App Using an External API

Now that you know how to use external libraries and APIs, let's build a simple **Weather App** that fetches real-time weather data using an external API. We'll use the `requests` library to interact with a public weather API.

Step-by-Step Code:

1. **Get an API Key:** To access weather data, sign up for a free account at OpenWeatherMap and get an API key.
2. **Install the `requests` Library:** If you haven't installed `requests`, you can install it with pip:

```
pip install requests
```

3. **Write the Weather App Code:**

```python
import requests

# Replace 'your_api_key' with your actual API key from OpenWeatherMap
API_KEY = 'your_api_key'
BASE_URL = "http://api.openweathermap.org/data/2.5/weather"

def get_weather(city):
    params = {
        'q': city,
        'appid': API_KEY,
        'units': 'metric'  # Use 'metric' for Celsius, 'imperial' for Fahrenheit
    }
    response = requests.get(BASE_URL, params=params)

    if response.status_code == 200:
        data = response.json()
```

```
        temperature = data['main']['temp']
        description = data['weather'][0]['description']
        print(f"The weather in {city} is {description} with a
temperature of {temperature}°C.")
    else:
        print("City not found. Please check the city name and try
again.")

def main():
    city = input("Enter the name of a city: ")
    get_weather(city)

if __name__ == "__main__":
    main()
```

Explanation of the Code:

- **API Request**: The `requests.get()` function sends a request to the OpenWeatherMap API using the city name provided by the user.
- **Parsing the Response**: If the city is found, the API returns a JSON response containing the weather details. We extract the temperature and weather description and display them.
- **Error Handling**: If the city is not found, the app displays an error message.

Example Interaction:

```
Enter the name of a city: Paris
The weather in Paris is clear sky with a temperature of 18.5°C.
```

9.6 What You Learned

In this chapter, you learned how to:

- Use **pip** to install external libraries.
- Work with popular libraries like **requests**, **NumPy**, and **Pandas**.
- Organize your code into **modules** for better maintainability.
- Build a **Weather App** that fetches real-time data from an external API using the `requests` library.

In the next chapter, we'll dive into **advanced file handling**, including working with binary files and file I/O operations.

This concludes **Chapter 9**! You've now gained the skills to extend Python's capabilities by using external libraries and organizing your code effectively. Keep exploring different libraries to discover the full power of Python!

Chapter 10: Advanced File Handling in Python

Overview: Working with Binary Files and File Operations

In earlier chapters, you learned how to handle simple text files using Python's built-in functions. Now, it's time to dive deeper into **advanced file handling**, which includes working with **binary files**, using Python's **file modes**, and dealing with **file I/O operations** efficiently. By mastering these concepts, you'll be able to manage large files, store complex data formats, and interact with files in a more powerful way.

By the end of this chapter, you'll be able to:

- Understand the difference between text files and binary files.
- Work with **file modes** to control how files are opened, read, written, and modified.
- Read and write **binary data**.
- Use **context managers** to handle files properly.
- Build a **File Backup Utility** that copies both text and binary files to a backup location.

10.1 Text Files vs. Binary Files

Before diving into the technical details, let's clarify the difference between **text files** and **binary files**:

Text Files:

- Text files store data in a human-readable format (e.g., `.txt`, `.csv`, `.json`).
- They contain characters (letters, numbers, symbols) encoded using character encoding such as UTF-8.
- You've already worked with text files in previous chapters (e.g., reading and writing plain text).

Binary Files:

- Binary files store data in a non-human-readable format, such as images, audio, videos, executables, or compiled programs.
- Data in binary files is stored as raw bytes (`0s` and `1s`).
- Common binary file formats include `.jpg`, `.png`, `.mp4`, `.exe`, and `.bin`.

In Python, the way you open and handle files depends on whether they are text or binary. Let's explore that in more detail.

10.2 File Modes

When working with files in Python, you need to specify **file modes** to control how the file will be opened. Some common file modes are:

Mode	Description
r	Open the file for reading (default).
w	Open the file for writing (overwrites if the file exists).
a	Open the file for appending (adds content to the end of the file).
rb	Open the file for reading in binary mode.
wb	Open the file for writing in binary mode.
r+	Open the file for both reading and writing.
x	Create a new file and open it for writing (fails if the file exists).

10.3 Working with Binary Files

To work with binary files, you must open them in **binary mode** by using the b character in the mode string (e.g., rb for reading or wb for writing). This ensures that Python treats the file's content as raw bytes.

Reading Binary Files

To read a binary file, you use the rb mode. Here's an example of reading an image file:

```python
with open("example.jpg", "rb") as file:
    binary_data = file.read()
    print(f"Read {len(binary_data)} bytes.")
```

In this example:

- The file example.jpg is opened in binary mode (rb).

- The `read()` method reads the entire file as a sequence of bytes.
- The length of the binary data (number of bytes) is displayed.

Writing Binary Files

To write binary data to a file, use the `wb` mode. Here's an example of writing binary data to a file:

```
binary_data = b"Hello, binary world!"
with open("output.bin", "wb") as file:
    file.write(binary_data)
    print("Binary data written to output.bin.")
```

In this case:

- The string `b"Hello, binary world!"` represents binary data (note the `b` prefix).
- The `write()` method writes the binary data to the file `output.bin`.

10.4 Buffered and Unbuffered File Operations

When reading or writing files, Python uses **buffered I/O** by default. This means that data is read from or written to a buffer (a temporary memory space) before it's passed to the file. Buffered operations are faster because they minimize disk access.

You can control the buffering behavior using the `buffering` parameter:

```
# No buffering (unbuffered)
with open("example.txt", "r", buffering=0) as file:
    data = file.read()
```

10.5 Using Context Managers for File Handling

Python's **context managers** (introduced using the `with` statement) are the best way to handle files because they ensure that files are properly closed after they are used, even if an error occurs during file operations.

You've already seen how to use context managers in earlier chapters:

```
with open("file.txt", "r") as file:
    data = file.read()
```

When using `with`, you don't need to call `file.close()` explicitly because the file is automatically closed once the code block finishes executing.

10.6 Working with Large Files

When working with very large files, it's inefficient (or impossible) to read the entire file into memory. In such cases, you can read the file in **chunks** or process it line by line.

Reading a File in Chunks

```
with open("largefile.txt", "r") as file:
    while chunk := file.read(1024):  # Read 1024 bytes at a time
        process(chunk)  # Perform some operation on the chunk
```

Reading a File Line by Line

You can read files line by line using a loop, which is useful for processing logs, large text files, or datasets.

```
with open("largefile.txt", "r") as file:
    for line in file:
        print(line.strip())  # Process each line
```

10.7 Handling File I/O Exceptions

Working with files involves dealing with potential errors such as missing files, read/write permission issues, or disk-related problems. Python provides several built-in exceptions to handle these scenarios:

- `FileNotFoundError`: Raised when trying to open a non-existent file.

```
try:
    with open("nonexistentfile.txt", "r") as file:
        data = file.read()
except FileNotFoundError:
    print("File not found!")
```

- `PermissionError`: Raised when you don't have permission to read or write a file.

```
try:
    with open("/root/secret.txt", "r") as file:
```

```
        data = file.read()
except PermissionError:
    print("Permission denied!")
```

- `IOError`: A more general exception for handling file input/output errors.

10.8 Building a File Backup Utility

Let's apply what you've learned by building a simple **File Backup Utility**. This utility will allow users to copy both text and binary files from one location to a backup folder.

Project: File Backup Utility

Overview

The **File Backup Utility** will:

1. Copy files from a specified source directory to a backup directory.
2. Handle both text and binary files.
3. Handle potential file-related errors (e.g., file not found, permission errors).

Step-by-Step Code

1. **Import Required Libraries**

```
import os
import shutil
```

2. **Define the Backup Function**

```
def backup_files(source_dir, backup_dir):
    # Ensure the backup directory exists
    os.makedirs(backup_dir, exist_ok=True)

    # Iterate over files in the source directory
    for filename in os.listdir(source_dir):
        source_file = os.path.join(source_dir, filename)
        backup_file = os.path.join(backup_dir, filename)

        # Skip directories, we only want to copy files
        if os.path.isfile(source_file):
```

```python
            try:
                shutil.copy2(source_file, backup_file)  # Copy file with metadata
                print(f"Copied: {source_file} to {backup_file}")
            except IOError as e:
                print(f"Error copying {source_file}: {e}")
            except Exception as e:
                print(f"Unexpected error: {e}")
```

3. **Main Program Function**

```python
def main():
    source_dir = input("Enter the source directory: ")
    backup_dir = input("Enter the backup directory: ")

    if not os.path.exists(source_dir):
        print("Source directory does not exist.")
        return

    backup_files(source_dir, backup_dir)
    print("Backup completed successfully.")

if __name__ == "__main__":
    main()
```

Final Code: File Backup Utility

Here's the complete code for your **File Backup Utility**:

```python
import os
import shutil

def backup_files(source_dir, backup_dir):
    os.makedirs(backup_dir, exist_ok=True)

    for filename in os.listdir(source_dir):
        source_file = os.path.join(source_dir, filename)
        backup_file = os.path.join(backup_dir, filename)

        if os.path.isfile(source_file):
            try:
```

```python
                shutil.copy2(source_file, backup_file)
                print(f"Copied: {source_file} to {backup_file}")
            except IOError as e:
                print(f"Error copying {source_file}: {e}")
            except Exception as e:
                print(f"Unexpected error: {e}")

def main():
    source_dir = input("Enter the source directory: ")
    backup_dir = input("Enter the backup directory: ")

    if not os.path.exists(source_dir):
        print("Source directory does not exist.")
        return

    backup_files(source_dir, backup_dir)
    print("Backup completed successfully.")

if __name__ == "__main__":
    main()
```

Example Interaction

```
Enter the source directory: /path/to/source
Enter the backup directory: /path/to/backup
Copied: /path/to/source/file1.txt to /path/to/backup/file1.txt
Copied: /path/to/source/image.jpg to /path/to/backup/image.jpg
Backup completed successfully.
```

10.9 What You Learned

In this chapter, you learned how to:

- Work with **binary files** in Python.
- Use different **file modes** to control file access.
- Read and write **large files** efficiently using chunked reads.
- Handle common **file I/O exceptions** like `FileNotFoundError` and `PermissionError`.
- Build a **File Backup Utility** that can copy both text and binary files while handling file-related errors.

In the next chapter, we'll explore **regular expressions** and how to use them for pattern matching in text.

This concludes **Chapter 10**! You're now equipped with advanced file handling techniques, allowing you to manage large datasets and binary data in your Python programs. Keep practicing to master these skills!

Chapter 11: Introduction to Regular Expressions (Regex)

Overview: Pattern Matching in Text with Regular Expressions

Regular expressions (commonly called **regex**) are a powerful tool for matching patterns in text. They allow you to search, extract, modify, and manipulate strings based on specific patterns. Whether you're parsing email addresses, phone numbers, or validating input, regex provides a flexible and efficient way to work with text.

In this chapter, you'll learn:

- The basics of regular expressions.
- How to create and use regex patterns.
- How to work with Python's built-in `re` module.
- Common use cases for regex.
- By the end of this chapter, you'll build a **Text Pattern Finder** to search for specific patterns in a file.

11.1 What Are Regular Expressions?

A **regular expression** (regex) is a special sequence of characters that defines a search pattern. You can think of regex as a **pattern-matching tool** for strings. You can use it to:

- Search for specific patterns in a string.
- Extract or replace parts of a string.
- Validate input formats (e.g., email addresses, phone numbers).

Basic Example:

Suppose you want to find all occurrences of the word "Python" in a paragraph. You could use the regex pattern `r"Python"` to match every instance of the word "Python".

```
import re

text = "I am learning Python. Python is fun!"
matches = re.findall(r"Python", text)
print(matches)  # Output: ['Python', 'Python']
```

In this example, `re.findall()` searches for all occurrences of the pattern `"Python"` in the text.

11.2 Working with Python's `re` Module

Python provides the `re` module to work with regular expressions. Here are some of the most commonly used functions:

Function	Description
`re.search()`	Searches for the first occurrence of a pattern in a string.
`re.findall()`	Returns all occurrences of a pattern in a string.
`re.match()`	Checks if a pattern matches the start of a string.
`re.sub()`	Replaces occurrences of a pattern in a string.
`re.split()`	Splits a string by occurrences of a pattern.

Let's explore these functions with some examples.

11.3 Basic Regex Patterns

Regex patterns are made up of **special characters** (called **metacharacters**) and **literal characters**. Here are some basic regex metacharacters:

Metacharacter	Description
.	Matches any character except a newline.
^	Matches the start of a string.
$	Matches the end of a string.
*	Matches 0 or more repetitions of the preceding character.

+	Matches 1 or more repetitions of the preceding character.
?	Matches 0 or 1 repetition of the preceding character.
[ ]	Matches any single character inside the brackets (character class).
\d	Matches any digit (0-9).
\w	Matches any word character (letters, digits, and underscores).
\s	Matches any whitespace character.

11.4 Common Regex Functions in Python

1. re.search()

`re.search()` scans through a string, looking for the first occurrence of a pattern. If a match is found, it returns a **match object**; otherwise, it returns `None`.

```
import re

text = "My email is example@mail.com"
match = re.search(r"\w+@\w+\.\w+", text)

if match:
    print(f"Email found: {match.group()}")  # Output: Email found: example@mail.com
```

In this example:

- The pattern `r"\w+@\w+\.\w+"` matches an email address format.
- `re.search()` finds the first match in the string and returns it.

2. re.findall()

`re.findall()` returns all occurrences of a pattern in a string as a list.

```
import re

text = "My phone numbers are 123-456-7890 and 987-654-3210"
```

```
matches = re.findall(r"\d{3}-\d{3}-\d{4}", text)
print(matches)   # Output: ['123-456-7890', '987-654-3210']
```

In this example, the pattern `r"\d{3}-\d{3}-\d{4}"` matches phone numbers in the format `123-456-7890`.

3. `re.sub()`

`re.sub()` replaces all occurrences of a pattern with a replacement string.

```
import re

text = "I love JavaScript. JavaScript is fun!"
new_text = re.sub(r"JavaScript", "Python", text)
print(new_text)   # Output: I love Python. Python is fun!
```

In this example, `re.sub()` replaces every occurrence of "JavaScript" with "Python".

4. `re.split()`

`re.split()` splits a string by the occurrences of a pattern.

```
import re

text = "apple, banana, cherry"
fruits = re.split(r",\s*", text)
print(fruits)   # Output: ['apple', 'banana', 'cherry']
```

Here, the pattern `r",\s*"` splits the string by commas and optional spaces.

11.5 Capturing Groups in Regex

Capturing groups allow you to extract specific parts of a match. Parentheses `()` are used to define groups.

Example: Extracting Date Components

Suppose you have dates in the format `YYYY-MM-DD`, and you want to extract the year, month, and day separately.

```
import re

text = "The event is on 2023-10-04."
```

```python
match = re.search(r"(\d{4})-(\d{2})-(\d{2})", text)

if match:
    year, month, day = match.groups()
    print(f"Year: {year}, Month: {month}, Day: {day}")
    # Output: Year: 2023, Month: 10, Day: 04
```

In this example:

- The pattern `r"(\d{4})-(\d{2})-(\d{2})"` defines three capturing groups: one for the year, one for the month, and one for the day.
- `match.groups()` returns a tuple containing the captured groups.

11.6 Regex Special Sequences

Regex includes several **special sequences** that are useful for matching common patterns:

Sequence	Description
\d	Matches any digit (equivalent to [0-9]).
\D	Matches any non-digit character.
\w	Matches any word character (letters, digits, and underscore).
\W	Matches any non-word character.
\s	Matches any whitespace character (spaces, tabs, newlines).
\S	Matches any non-whitespace character.

Example: Matching Alphanumeric Strings

```python
import re

text = "The code is ABC123."
match = re.search(r"\w{3}\d{3}", text)
```

```
if match:
    print(f"Alphanumeric code found: {match.group()}")   # Output:
Alphanumeric code found: ABC123
```

Here, \w{3} matches three word characters, and \d{3} matches three digits.

11.7 Regex Flags

Python's re module provides several **flags** that modify the behavior of regex functions. Some common flags are:

Flag	Description
re.IGNORECASE (re.I)	Makes the pattern case-insensitive.
re.MULTILINE (re.M)	Allows ^ and $ to match the start and end of each line, not just the entire string.
re.DOTALL (re.S)	Makes the dot (.) match newline characters as well.

Example: Case-Insensitive Matching

```
import re

text = "Python is fun. python is powerful."
matches = re.findall(r"python", text, re.IGNORECASE)
print(matches)   # Output: ['Python', 'python']
```

In this example, re.IGNORECASE allows the pattern to match "Python" and "python" regardless of case.

11.8 Practical Applications of Regex

Let's explore some common use cases where regex shines:

1. Validating Email Addresses

```
import re
```

```python
email = "user@example.com"
if re.match(r"[^@]+@[^@]+\.[^@]+", email):
    print("Valid email address")
else:
    print("Invalid email address")
```

2. Finding URLs in a Text

```python
import re

text = "Visit https://www.example.com or http://example.org for more info."
urls = re.findall(r"https?://\S+", text)
print(urls)   # Output: ['https://www.example.com', 'http://example.org']
```

3. Extracting Phone Numbers

```python
import re

text = "Call me at (555) 123-4567 or 555-987-6543."
phone_numbers = re.findall(r"\(?\d{3}\)?[-.\s]?\d{3}[-.\s]?\d{4}", text)
print(phone_numbers)   # Output: ['(555) 123-4567', '555-987-6543']
```

11.9 Building a Text Pattern Finder

Let's apply what you've learned by building a **Text Pattern Finder**. This program will search for specific patterns in a text file and display the results.

Project: Text Pattern Finder

Overview

The **Text Pattern Finder** will:

1. Prompt the user for a regex pattern.
2. Search a text file for all occurrences of the pattern.
3. Display the matching lines along with the matched text.

Step-by-Step Code

1. **Import Required Libraries**

```python
import re
```

2. **Define the Pattern Finder Function**

```python
def find_pattern_in_file(pattern, filename):
    try:
        with open(filename, "r") as file:
            for line_number, line in enumerate(file, 1):
                matches = re.findall(pattern, line)
                if matches:
                    print(f"Line {line_number}: {line.strip()}")
                    print(f"Matches: {matches}")
    except FileNotFoundError:
        print(f"File '{filename}' not found.")
```

3. **Main Program Function**

```python
def main():
    filename = input("Enter the filename: ")
    pattern = input("Enter the regex pattern: ")

    print(f"\nSearching for pattern '{pattern}' in '{filename}':")
    find_pattern_in_file(pattern, filename)

if __name__ == "__main__":
    main()
```

Final Code: Text Pattern Finder

Here's the complete code for your **Text Pattern Finder**:

```python
import re

def find_pattern_in_file(pattern, filename):
    try:
        with open(filename, "r") as file:
            for line_number, line in enumerate(file, 1):
                matches = re.findall(pattern, line)
                if matches:
                    print(f"Line {line_number}: {line.strip()}")
                    print(f"Matches: {matches}")
```

```
    except FileNotFoundError:
        print(f"File '{filename}' not found.")

def main():
    filename = input("Enter the filename: ")
    pattern = input("Enter the regex pattern: ")

    print(f"\nSearching for pattern '{pattern}' in '{filename}':")
    find_pattern_in_file(pattern, filename)

if __name__ == "__main__":
    main()
```

Example Interaction

```
Enter the filename: example.txt
Enter the regex pattern: \d{3}-\d{3}-\d{4}

Searching for pattern '\d{3}-\d{3}-\d{4}' in 'example.txt':
Line 5: Contact: 123-456-7890
Matches: ['123-456-7890']
```

11.10 What You Learned

In this chapter, you learned:

- The basics of **regular expressions** and how to create regex patterns.
- How to use Python's `re` **module** to search, extract, and replace patterns in text.
- Common regex use cases, including validating emails and finding phone numbers.
- How to build a **Text Pattern Finder** to search for regex patterns in a file.

In the next chapter, we'll dive into **web scraping** and learn how to extract data from websites using Python.

This concludes **Chapter 11**! You now have a solid understanding of regex and its practical applications. Keep practicing with different patterns to become proficient in pattern matching with regular expressions!

Chapter 12: GUI Programming with Tkinter

Overview: Adding Graphical User Interfaces to Python Applications

So far, we've worked with Python programs that interact through the command line. However, many real-world applications feature **Graphical User Interfaces (GUIs)**, allowing users to interact with the software in a more intuitive way. GUIs offer buttons, labels, input fields, and other elements that make applications easier to use.

In this chapter, you will learn how to create **GUIs** using Python's built-in **Tkinter** library. Tkinter provides a fast and simple way to build graphical applications in Python, without the need for complex external libraries. By the end of this chapter, you will build a simple **Weather App** that takes user input and displays weather data.

12.1 Introduction to Tkinter

Tkinter is the standard Python library for building GUI applications. It provides various tools (called **widgets**) to create windows, buttons, text fields, labels, and more. Tkinter is a wrapper around the **Tk GUI toolkit**, which is available on most platforms, making it cross-platform.

Tkinter is well suited for small to medium desktop applications and offers everything you need to build functional graphical interfaces.

Importing Tkinter

To start working with Tkinter, you need to import the library:

```
import tkinter as tk
```

Alternatively, you can import specific parts of the library:

```
from tkinter import Button, Label, Entry
```

12.2 Creating Windows and Widgets

A **widget** in Tkinter is an element of the GUI, such as a button, label, or input field. Tkinter offers many widget types that you can add to a window.

Creating a Basic Window

Here's how to create a simple window using Tkinter:

```python
import tkinter as tk

# Create a window
window = tk.Tk()
window.title("My First GUI")

# Start the GUI event loop
window.mainloop()
```

In this code:

- `tk.Tk()` creates the main application window.
- `title()` sets the window's title.
- `mainloop()` keeps the window open, waiting for user interaction.

Adding Widgets: Buttons, Labels, and Input Fields

Once the window is created, you can start adding **widgets** to it. Common widgets include **labels** (for displaying text), **buttons** (for handling user clicks), and **entry fields** (for user input).

```python
import tkinter as tk

# Create a window
window = tk.Tk()
window.title("Widget Example")

# Add a label widget
label = tk.Label(window, text="Enter your name:")
label.pack()  # Pack the widget into the window

# Add an input field (Entry widget)
entry = tk.Entry(window)
entry.pack()

# Add a button widget
button = tk.Button(window, text="Submit")
button.pack()

# Start the GUI event loop
window.mainloop()
```

Explanation:

- **Label**: Displays static text (`Label(window, text="Enter your name:")`).
- **Entry**: An input field for user input.
- **Button**: A clickable button that can trigger events (we'll cover event handling next).

Widgets are added to the window using the `pack()` method, which automatically places them in the window.

12.3 Handling Events in Tkinter

GUI applications are **event-driven**. This means they respond to events like button clicks, key presses, or text input. In Tkinter, you handle events by attaching **callbacks** (functions that run in response to events) to widgets.

Handling Button Clicks

To handle a button click, you attach a function (callback) to the button's `command` parameter.

```python
import tkinter as tk

def on_button_click():
    user_input = entry.get()  # Get the input from the entry field
    label.config(text=f"Hello, {user_input}!")  # Update the label text

# Create a window
window = tk.Tk()
window.title("Event Handling Example")

# Add a label
label = tk.Label(window, text="Enter your name:")
label.pack()

# Add an entry field
entry = tk.Entry(window)
entry.pack()

# Add a button with event handling
button = tk.Button(window, text="Submit", command=on_button_click)
```

```
button.pack()

# Start the event loop
window.mainloop()
```

Explanation:

- **Callback Function**: The function `on_button_click()` is executed when the button is clicked. It retrieves the text from the entry field using `entry.get()` and updates the label using `label.config()`.
- **command Parameter**: You pass the `on_button_click` function to the button using `command=on_button_click`. This function is called whenever the button is pressed.

12.4 Laying Out a GUI Application

Tkinter provides multiple ways to arrange widgets in the window:

1. **pack()**: Places widgets vertically or horizontally.
2. **grid()**: Organizes widgets in a grid layout (rows and columns).
3. **place()**: Positions widgets at an exact coordinate.

Using the `grid()` Layout

The `grid()` method arranges widgets in a grid of rows and columns. Here's an example:

```
import tkinter as tk

# Create a window
window = tk.Tk()
window.title("Grid Layout Example")

# Add widgets using grid
tk.Label(window, text="Name:").grid(row=0, column=0)
tk.Entry(window).grid(row=0, column=1)

tk.Label(window, text="Age:").grid(row=1, column=0)
tk.Entry(window).grid(row=1, column=1)

# Add a submit button
tk.Button(window, text="Submit").grid(row=2, column=0,
columnspan=2)
```

```
# Start the event loop
window.mainloop()
```

Explanation:

- `grid(row, column)`: Places widgets in a grid of rows and columns. In this example, the labels and entry fields are placed in rows 0 and 1, while the button spans across two columns using `columnspan=2`.

12.5 Key Concepts in Tkinter

1. Building Interactive Applications

Tkinter allows you to create interactive applications that respond to user input. Widgets like buttons, entry fields, and sliders let users interact with your program, and you can handle their actions using event-driven programming.

2. Organizing GUI Elements

You can arrange and organize GUI elements (widgets) using layout managers like `pack()`, `grid()`, and `place()`. Each has its strengths:

- `pack()` is simple and arranges widgets vertically or horizontally.
- `grid()` is more flexible for complex layouts.
- `place()` is useful for precise positioning.

3. Basics of Event-Driven Programming

Tkinter applications follow an **event-driven programming model**. This means that the application is constantly waiting for user actions (events), such as button clicks or text input, and responds by calling event-handling functions (callbacks).

12.6 Project: Building a Simple Weather App Using Tkinter

Let's put everything together and build a simple **Weather App** using Tkinter. The app will take user input (a city name) and display placeholder weather data. For advanced users, you can extend the project to fetch live weather data from an API.

Step-by-Step Code: Simple Weather App

1. **Create the GUI Window and Widgets**

```python
import tkinter as tk

def show_weather():
    city = entry.get()
    label.config(text=f"Weather in {city}: Sunny, 25°C")  # Placeholder weather data

# Create the main window
window = tk.Tk()
window.title("Weather App")

# Create a label for instructions
instruction_label = tk.Label(window, text="Enter city name:")
instruction_label.pack()

# Create an entry widget for city input
entry = tk.Entry(window)
entry.pack()

# Create a button to show weather data
button = tk.Button(window, text="Show Weather", command=show_weather)
button.pack()

# Create a label to display the weather information
label = tk.Label(window, text="")
label.pack()

# Start the event loop
window.mainloop()
```

2. **Explanation**:
   - The user enters a city name into the entry widget.
   - When the button is clicked, the show_weather() function is called. It updates the label with placeholder weather information.

Basic Features:

- **Entry Field**: For users to input the city name.
- **Button**: Triggers the display of weather data.
- **Label**: Displays the weather information.

Advanced Option: Fetching Weather Data from an API

For more advanced users, you can modify the app to fetch real weather data from an API like **OpenWeatherMap**.

Steps:

1. Sign up for a free API key at OpenWeatherMap.
2. Install the `requests` library to fetch data from the API:

```
pip install requests
```

3. Modify the `show_weather()` function to fetch real-time weather data:

```python
import requests
import tkinter as tk

API_KEY = 'your_api_key_here'
BASE_URL = "http://api.openweathermap.org/data/2.5/weather"

def show_weather():
    city = entry.get()
    params = {
        'q': city,
        'appid': API_KEY,
        'units': 'metric'
    }
    response = requests.get(BASE_URL, params=params)
    if response.status_code == 200:
        data = response.json()
        temperature = data['main']['temp']
        description = data['weather'][0]['description']
        label.config(text=f"Weather in {city}: {description}, {temperature}°C")
    else:
        label.config(text="City not found")

# GUI setup remains the same as before
window = tk.Tk()
window.title("Weather App")
instruction_label = tk.Label(window, text="Enter city name:")
instruction_label.pack()
entry = tk.Entry(window)
entry.pack()
```

```
button = tk.Button(window, text="Show Weather",
command=show_weather)
button.pack()
label = tk.Label(window, text="")
label.pack()
window.mainloop()
```

12.7 What You Learned

In this chapter, you learned how to:

- Use **Tkinter** to create GUI applications.
- Add and arrange **widgets** like buttons, labels, and input fields.
- Handle **events** like button clicks to create interactive applications.
- Build a simple **Weather App** that displays weather information based on user input.

In the next chapter, we'll dive into **web scraping** and learn how to extract data from websites using Python.

Chapter 13: Capstone Project – Build a Simple Game

Overview: Applying Everything You've Learned

You've made it to the capstone chapter! In this final project, you'll put together everything you've learned throughout the book by building a simple **Quiz Game**. This project will reinforce key concepts such as:

- Control flow
- Functions
- Object-Oriented Programming (OOP)
- Error handling
- File operations

We'll also introduce you to the basics of **game programming** using the **pygame** library for those interested in adding a graphical interface. By the end of this chapter, you'll have built an interactive quiz game that asks trivia questions, keeps track of the score, and provides feedback.

13.1 Recap of Major Concepts

Before diving into game programming, let's briefly recap the key concepts that we'll apply in this project.

Control Flow

- **Conditional Statements** (`if`, `else`, `elif`) allow the program to take different actions based on certain conditions.
- **Loops** (`for`, `while`) allow the program to repeat actions multiple times, which is essential in game logic.

Functions

- Functions allow you to break down complex problems into smaller, reusable blocks of code.
- **Parameters** and **return values** help in passing data to and from functions.

Object-Oriented Programming (OOP)

- **Classes** allow you to model entities (e.g., a `Question` object) with attributes and methods.
- **Inheritance** can be used to extend functionality from a base class.

Error Handling

- Using `try-except` blocks helps handle unexpected situations, such as invalid input from the user or missing files.

File Operations

- Reading and writing files allows the game to load quiz questions from a file and store the player's score.

13.2 Introduction to Game Programming Basics

Python offers various libraries for game development, and one of the most popular is **pygame**. While building complex games like 3D shooters might be out of scope for this book, pygame makes it easy to build 2D games with graphics, sound, and user input.

We'll cover the basics of pygame in the **advanced option** of this chapter, but for now, let's focus on building a command-line-based quiz game.

13.3 Project: Building a Simple Quiz Game

Overview

In this project, you'll create a **Quiz Game** where the user is asked trivia questions, and their answers are evaluated. The game will:

1. Load trivia questions from a file.
2. Ask the player multiple-choice questions.
3. Keep track of the player's score.
4. Provide feedback based on correct or incorrect answers.

Step-by-Step Code

1. **Creating the Question Class**

First, we'll create a `Question` class that holds the trivia question, its possible answers, and the correct answer.

```
class Question:
    def __init__(self, text, choices, correct_answer):
        self.text = text
        self.choices = choices
        self.correct_answer = correct_answer
```

```python
def is_correct(self, answer):
    return answer.lower() == self.correct_answer.lower()
```

Explanation:

- The `Question` class has three attributes: the question text, the possible choices, and the correct answer.
- The `is_correct()` method checks if the user's answer matches the correct answer.
2. **Loading Questions from a File**

We'll load trivia questions from a file. Each question will be stored in a text file in the format:

```
What is the capital of France?
a. Paris
b. London
c. Berlin
d. Madrid
a
```

Here's the code to read questions from a file and create `Question` objects:

```python
def load_questions(filename):
    questions = []
    try:
        with open(filename, 'r') as file:
            lines = file.readlines()
            for i in range(0, len(lines), 6):
                text = lines[i].strip()
                choices = [lines[i+1].strip(), lines[i+2].strip(), lines[i+3].strip(), lines[i+4].strip()]
                correct_answer = lines[i+5].strip()
                question = Question(text, choices, correct_answer)
                questions.append(question)
    except FileNotFoundError:
        print(f"Error: The file '{filename}' was not found.")
    return questions
```

Explanation:

- `load_questions()` reads the file and creates `Question` objects. It processes each question in blocks of six lines (the question, four choices, and the correct answer).

3. **Asking the User Trivia Questions**

Next, we'll create a function to ask the player a question, display the possible answers, and evaluate their response.

```python
def ask_question(question):
    print(question.text)
    for i, choice in enumerate(question.choices, start=1):
        print(f"{i}. {choice}")
    answer = input("Your answer (a/b/c/d): ")
    if question.is_correct(answer):
        print("Correct!\n")
        return True
    else:
        print(f"Incorrect! The correct answer was: {question.correct_answer}\n")
        return False
```

Explanation:

- The `ask_question()` function displays the question and choices, then checks if the user's answer is correct using the `is_correct()` method.

4. **Keeping Track of the Score**

Let's create the game loop where we ask the player multiple questions and keep track of their score.

```python
def play_quiz(questions):
    score = 0
    for question in questions:
        if ask_question(question):
            score += 1
    print(f"\nYour final score is {score}/{len(questions)}.")
```

Explanation:

- `play_quiz()` loops through all the questions, calls `ask_question()`, and increments the score if the player answers correctly.

5. **Main Program Function**

Finally, we'll tie everything together in the `main()` function:

```python
def main():
    print("Welcome to the Quiz Game!")
    filename = input("Enter the name of the question file: ")
```

```python
        questions = load_questions(filename)

    if questions:
        play_quiz(questions)
    else:
        print("No questions available. Exiting.")
```

Full Code:

Here's the complete code for the **Quiz Game**:

```python
class Question:
    def __init__(self, text, choices, correct_answer):
        self.text = text
        self.choices = choices
        self.correct_answer = correct_answer

    def is_correct(self, answer):
        return answer.lower() == self.correct_answer.lower()

def load_questions(filename):
    questions = []
    try:
        with open(filename, 'r') as file:
            lines = file.readlines()
            for i in range(0, len(lines), 6):
                text = lines[i].strip()
                choices = [lines[i+1].strip(), lines[i+2].strip(), lines[i+3].strip(), lines[i+4].strip()]
                correct_answer = lines[i+5].strip()
                question = Question(text, choices, correct_answer)
                questions.append(question)
    except FileNotFoundError:
        print(f"Error: The file '{filename}' was not found.")
    return questions

def ask_question(question):
    print(question.text)
    for i, choice in enumerate(question.choices, start=1):
        print(f"{i}. {choice}")
    answer = input("Your answer (a/b/c/d): ")
    if question.is_correct(answer):
        print("Correct!\n")
```

```python
            return True
        else:
            print(f"Incorrect! The correct answer was: {question.correct_answer}\n")
            return False

def play_quiz(questions):
    score = 0
    for question in questions:
        if ask_question(question):
            score += 1
    print(f"\nYour final score is {score}/{len(questions)}.")

def main():
    print("Welcome to the Quiz Game!")
    filename = input("Enter the name of the question file: ")
    questions = load_questions(filename)

    if questions:
        play_quiz(questions)
    else:
        print("No questions available. Exiting.")

if __name__ == "__main__":
    main()
```

13.4 Advanced Option: Adding a GUI with Pygame

For advanced users, you can add a graphical interface to the quiz game using **pygame**. Here's a simple overview of how to use pygame for displaying the quiz questions, handling input, and showing feedback.

1. **Install pygame**:

```
pip install pygame
```

2. **Basic Game Loop in Pygame**:
    - Create the game window.
    - Display the questions and answers.
    - Capture user input (keyboard or mouse clicks).
    - Update the score based on correct answers.

13.5 What You Learned

In this chapter, you:

- Built a complete **Quiz Game** that reinforces control flow, functions, OOP, and file handling.
- Learned how to load and process questions from a file.
- Optionally explored adding a graphical interface using **pygame**.

This concludes your journey through the book! By completing this capstone project, you've applied core programming concepts in a fun and practical way. Keep building, experimenting, and expanding your knowledge to tackle even more exciting projects in the future!

Chapter 14: Where to Go from Here – Expanding Your Python Knowledge

Overview: Next Steps in Python Programming

Congratulations on reaching the final chapter of this book! You've come a long way, mastering the basics of Python programming, learning how to build projects, and applying advanced concepts like file handling, object-oriented programming (OOP), and graphical interfaces. Now that you've built a strong foundation, it's time to look ahead to what you can explore next.

In this chapter, we'll discuss some exciting libraries and frameworks that will help you take your Python skills to the next level. We'll also explore online resources for continued learning, best practices for writing efficient and clean Python code, and introduce you to **version control** with **Git** and **GitHub**.

14.1 Recommended Libraries and Frameworks

Python's true power lies in its vast ecosystem of libraries and frameworks, each designed to address specific needs. Whether you're interested in web development, data science, machine learning, or automation, Python has something for everyone.

1. Web Development Frameworks: Django and Flask

If you're interested in building web applications, **Django** and **Flask** are two of the most popular web frameworks in Python.

Django

- **Overview**: Django is a high-level web framework that encourages rapid development and clean, pragmatic design. It follows the **Model-View-Controller (MVC)** architectural pattern and provides built-in features like an admin interface, user authentication, and database management.
- **When to use it**: Use Django for large, complex web applications that require a lot of built-in functionality.
- **Learn more**: Django Official Website

Flask

- **Overview**: Flask is a lightweight, minimalistic web framework that gives you more control over how you structure your application. It's ideal for building smaller web apps or APIs and gives developers more flexibility compared to Django.

- **When to use it**: Use Flask for smaller projects or if you want more control over the components of your web app.
- **Learn more**: Flask Official Website

2. Data Science and Machine Learning: Pandas, NumPy, and Scikit-learn

If you're interested in **data science**, **data analysis**, or **machine learning**, Python offers powerful libraries like **Pandas**, **NumPy**, and **Scikit-learn**.

Pandas

- **Overview**: Pandas is the go-to library for data manipulation and analysis. It provides data structures like **DataFrames** for organizing and analyzing structured data, such as Excel files or databases.
- **When to use it**: Use Pandas for data wrangling, cleaning, and analysis in data science projects.
- **Learn more**: Pandas Documentation

NumPy

- **Overview**: NumPy is the fundamental package for scientific computing in Python. It provides support for multi-dimensional arrays and matrices, along with a collection of mathematical functions to operate on these arrays.
- **When to use it**: Use NumPy for numerical computations, matrix operations, and working with large datasets.
- **Learn more**: NumPy Documentation

Scikit-learn

- **Overview**: Scikit-learn is one of the most popular machine learning libraries. It offers simple and efficient tools for data mining, data analysis, and machine learning.
- **When to use it**: Use Scikit-learn to build machine learning models like decision trees, linear regression, clustering algorithms, and more.
- **Learn more**: Scikit-learn Documentation

3. Automation: Selenium and BeautifulSoup

If you want to automate web-related tasks, like filling forms or scraping data from websites, **Selenium** and **BeautifulSoup** are excellent libraries.

Selenium

- **Overview**: Selenium is used for automating web browsers. It allows you to programmatically interact with web pages by simulating user actions like clicking buttons, filling forms, and navigating through pages.
- **When to use it**: Use Selenium for web automation tasks like testing web applications or automating repetitive browser tasks.
- **Learn more**: Selenium Documentation

BeautifulSoup

- **Overview**: BeautifulSoup is a library for web scraping. It helps you extract and parse data from HTML or XML documents.
- **When to use it**: Use BeautifulSoup for scraping data from websites and converting it into structured formats.
- **Learn more**: BeautifulSoup Documentation

14.2 Online Resources and Communities for Continued Learning

There's always more to learn in the world of Python, and luckily, there are many online resources to help you continue your journey.

1. Python Documentation

- The official Python documentation is an invaluable resource for learning about specific modules, functions, and features. It provides detailed explanations of Python's syntax and built-in libraries.
- **Website**: Python Documentation

2. Stack Overflow

- Stack Overflow is a massive online community where developers can ask questions, share solutions, and collaborate on coding challenges. If you encounter issues or need clarification on Python-related topics, Stack Overflow is a great place to start.
- **Website**: Stack Overflow Python

3. Real Python

- Real Python offers high-quality Python tutorials, articles, and learning resources. Topics range from beginner to advanced levels, covering a wide range of Python libraries and applications.
- **Website**: Real Python

4. Python Discord

- Python Discord is a large and active online community of Python developers. It's a great place to meet other learners, ask questions, and participate in Python-related events and challenges.
- **Website**: Python Discord

5. FreeCodeCamp

- FreeCodeCamp offers free coding tutorials and projects, including Python-focused lessons. They also have a supportive community that helps learners through challenges.
- **Website**: FreeCodeCamp Python

14.3 Best Practices for Writing Clean and Efficient Python Code

As you become a more advanced Python programmer, writing **clean**, **efficient**, and **maintainable** code becomes increasingly important. Here are some best practices to follow:

1. Follow PEP 8 Guidelines

- **PEP 8** is the official Python style guide that outlines conventions for writing readable and consistent code. Following PEP 8 makes your code easier to read and share with others.
- Key practices include proper indentation, meaningful variable names, and consistent formatting.
- **Learn more**: PEP 8 – Python Style Guide

2. Use Descriptive Variable Names

- Avoid cryptic variable names like `x` or `a`. Instead, use descriptive names that reflect the purpose of the variable. For example, `total_price` is much clearer than `tp`.

3. Keep Functions Small and Focused

- Each function should have a single, well-defined purpose. If a function is doing too many things, consider breaking it up into smaller functions.

4. Write Documentation and Comments

- Use docstrings to document your functions and modules. Comments are useful for explaining why certain decisions were made in the code, especially for complex logic.

5. Use List Comprehensions and Generators

- Python provides powerful features like **list comprehensions** and **generators** that allow you to write more concise and efficient code.
- Example:

```python
# List comprehension to create a list of squares
squares = [x ** 2 for x in range(10)]
```

6. Handle Errors Gracefully

- Use **try-except** blocks to handle exceptions and errors gracefully, rather than letting your program crash. Be specific about the exceptions you handle and provide useful error messages.

7. Write Unit Tests

- Testing is a crucial part of writing reliable software. Python's `unittest` module allows you to write test cases that ensure your functions behave as expected.

14.4 Introduction to Version Control with Git and GitHub

As you work on more projects, especially in collaboration with others, it's important to track changes in your code and collaborate efficiently. This is where **version control** systems like **Git** and platforms like **GitHub** come into play.

1. What is Git?

- **Git** is a version control system that tracks changes in your code over time. It allows you to manage different versions of your project, collaborate with others, and roll back to previous versions if needed.

2. What is GitHub?

- **GitHub** is a platform built on top of Git that allows you to store your repositories online, collaborate with others, and showcase your projects. GitHub is widely used in the industry and is a great way to manage your personal projects or contribute to open-source projects.

Basic Git Commands

Here's a quick overview of basic Git commands to get you started:

- `git init`: Initialize a new Git repository in your project folder.
- `git add`: Stage changes for the next commit.
- `git commit -m "message"`: Commit the staged changes with a descriptive message.
- `git push`: Push your changes to a remote repository (like GitHub).
- `git pull`: Pull the latest changes from a remote repository.

Setting Up a GitHub Repository

1. **Create a GitHub account**: Visit [GitHub](https://github.com) and sign up for a free account.
2. **Create a new repository**: Once logged in, click the "New Repository" button and follow the prompts to create a repository for your project.
3. **Push your code to GitHub**: After creating the repository, use Git commands (`git init`, `git add`, `git commit`, `git push`) to upload your project to GitHub.

Learn More About Git and GitHub

- [Git Documentation (https://git-scm.com/doc)](https://git-scm.com/doc)
- [GitHub Guides (https://guides.github.com/)](https://guides.github.com/)

14.5 Conclusion

You've completed an incredible journey from learning Python basics to building complex applications and games. But this is only the beginning! Python is a language with endless possibilities, and by exploring the libraries, frameworks, and tools mentioned in this chapter, you can expand your knowledge and skills in many exciting directions.

Here's a recap of what to focus on next:

1. **Explore advanced Python libraries**: Start with Django, Flask, Pandas, or Scikit-learn based on your interests.
2. **Join online communities**: Engage with the Python community on platforms like Stack Overflow, Reddit, or Python Discord.
3. **Adopt best practices**: Write clean, efficient code, and document your work.
4. **Learn Git and GitHub**: Start version controlling your projects and contributing to open-source software.

Congratulations on finishing this book! Keep learning, keep coding, and keep building amazing things with Python!

Appendices

Appendix A: Python Reference Sheet

This reference sheet contains a collection of commonly used Python functions, methods, and syntax to help you quickly look up frequently used concepts. Keep it handy as a quick guide while coding!

1. Common Python Functions

- `print()`: Prints output to the console.
  Example:

```
print("Hello, World!")
```

- `input()`: Reads input from the user.
  Example:

```
name = input("Enter your name: ")
```

- `len()`: Returns the length of an object.
  Example:

```
len([1, 2, 3])   # Output: 3
```

- `type()`: Returns the type of an object.
  Example:

```
type(42)   # Output: <class 'int'>
```

- `range()`: Generates a sequence of numbers.
  Example:

```
range(0, 5)   # Generates numbers from 0 to 4
```

- `int()`, `float()`, `str()`: Converts a value to an integer, float, or string.
  Example:

```
int("123")       # Output: 123
float("12.34")   # Output: 12.34
```

```python
str(42)   # Output: "42"
```

- `sum()`: Returns the sum of elements in an iterable.
  Example:

```python
sum([1, 2, 3])   # Output: 6
```

- `min()`, `max()`: Returns the minimum or maximum value in an iterable.
  Example:

```python
min([1, 2, 3])   # Output: 1
max([1, 2, 3])   # Output: 3
```

- `sorted()`: Returns a sorted list of items.
  Example:

```python
sorted([3, 1, 2])   # Output: [1, 2, 3]
```

---

2. List Methods

- `append()`: Adds an element to the end of the list.
  Example:

```python
lst = [1, 2, 3]
lst.append(4)   # lst is now [1, 2, 3, 4]
```

- `insert()`: Inserts an element at a specific index.
  Example:

```python
lst = [1, 3, 4]
lst.insert(1, 2)   # lst is now [1, 2, 3, 4]
```

- `remove()`: Removes the first occurrence of an element.
  Example:

```python
lst = [1, 2, 3, 2]
lst.remove(2)   # lst is now [1, 3, 2]
```

- `pop()`: Removes and returns the element at the specified position.
  Example:

```
lst = [1, 2, 3]
lst.pop()   # Returns 3, lst is now [1, 2]
```

- `clear()`: Removes all elements from the list.
  Example:

```
lst = [1, 2, 3]
lst.clear()   # lst is now []
```

- `index()`: Returns the index of the first occurrence of an element.
  Example:

```
lst = [1, 2, 3]
lst.index(2)   # Output: 1
```

- `count()`: Returns the number of occurrences of an element.
  Example:

```
lst = [1, 2, 2, 3]
lst.count(2)   # Output: 2
```

- `sort()`: Sorts the list in ascending order.
  Example:

```
lst = [3, 1, 2]
lst.sort()   # lst is now [1, 2, 3]
```

- `reverse()`: Reverses the order of the list.
  Example:

```
lst = [1, 2, 3]
lst.reverse()   # lst is now [3, 2, 1]
```

---

3. Dictionary Methods

- `get()`: Returns the value for a given key.
  Example:

```
dct = {"a": 1, "b": 2}
dct.get("a")   # Output: 1
```

- `keys()`: Returns a view object containing all the keys in the dictionary.
  Example:

```python
dct = {"a": 1, "b": 2}
dct.keys()   # Output: dict_keys(['a', 'b'])
```

- `values()`: Returns a view object containing all the values in the dictionary.
  Example:

```python
dct = {"a": 1, "b": 2}
dct.values()  # Output: dict_values([1, 2])
```

- `items()`: Returns a view object containing all key-value pairs.
  Example:

```python
dct = {"a": 1, "b": 2}
dct.items()   # Output: dict_items([('a', 1), ('b', 2)])
```

- `pop()`: Removes and returns the value for a given key.
  Example:

```python
dct = {"a": 1, "b": 2}
dct.pop("a")   # Output: 1, dct is now {"b": 2}
```

- `update()`: Updates the dictionary with key-value pairs from another dictionary.
  Example:

```python
dct = {"a": 1}
dct.update({"b": 2})   # dct is now {"a": 1, "b": 2}
```

- `clear()`: Removes all items from the dictionary.
  Example:

```python
dct = {"a": 1, "b": 2}
dct.clear()   # dct is now {}
```

4. String Methods

- `lower()`: Converts the string to lowercase.
  Example:

```
"HELLO".lower()   # Output: "hello"
```

- `upper()`: Converts the string to uppercase.
  Example:

```
"hello".upper()   # Output: "HELLO"
```

- `strip()`: Removes leading and trailing whitespace.
  Example:

```
"  Hello  ".strip()   # Output: "Hello"
```

- `split()`: Splits the string into a list of substrings.
  Example:

```
"a,b,c".split(",")   # Output: ['a', 'b', 'c']
```

- `replace()`: Replaces occurrences of a substring.
  Example:

```
"Hello".replace("H", "J")   # Output: "Jello"
```

- `find()`: Returns the index of the first occurrence of a substring.
  Example:

```
"hello".find("e")   # Output: 1
```

- `join()`: Joins elements of a list into a string, with a separator.
  Example:

```
",".join(["a", "b", "c"])   # Output: "a,b,c"
```

---

5. Control Flow Syntax

- `if`: Executes a block of code if the condition is `True`.
  Example:

```
if x > 5:
    print("x is greater than 5")
```

- `elif`: Adds another condition to the `if` statement.
  Example:

```
if x > 5:
    print("greater")
elif x == 5:
    print("equal")
```

- `else`: Executes if none of the `if` or `elif` conditions are `True`.
  Example:

```
if x > 5:
    print("greater")
else:
    print("less or equal")
```

- `for`: Loops through a sequence (list, range, etc.).
  Example:

```
for i in range(3):
    print(i)
```

- `while`: Repeats a block of code while the condition is `True`.
  Example:

```
while x < 5:
    x += 1
```

- `break`: Exits the current loop.
  Example:

```
for i in range(5):
    if i == 3:
        break
```

- `continue`: Skips the rest of the current iteration and moves to the next.
  Example:

```
for i in range(5):
    if i == 2:
        continue
    print(i)
```

- `try`/`except`: Handles exceptions and errors in code.
  Example:

```
try:
    x = 1 / 0
except ZeroDivisionError:
    print("Cannot divide by zero!")
```

Appendix B: Setting Up Python for Advanced Projects

As your projects grow in complexity, managing dependencies and setting up your development environment becomes essential. Here, we'll cover how to use **virtual environments**, manage packages with **pip**, and maintain a clean project structure.

1. Virtual Environments

A **virtual environment** is an isolated Python environment that allows you to manage project-specific dependencies without interfering with other projects. It ensures that each project can have its own package versions.

Creating a Virtual Environment

1. Navigate to your project directory.

Run the following command to create a virtual environment:

```
python -m venv venv
```

2. This creates a `venv` folder in your project directory.

Activating the Virtual Environment

- On **Windows**:

```
venv\Scripts\activate
```

- On **macOS/Linux**:

```
source venv/bin/activate
```

You should see (venv) in your terminal, indicating that the virtual environment is active.

Deactivating the Virtual Environment

To deactivate the virtual environment, simply run:

```
deactivate
```

2. Package Management with pip

pip is Python's package installer, and it allows you to install, upgrade, and remove Python packages.

Installing a Package

To install a package, use the following command:

```
pip install package_name
```

Example:

```
pip install requests
```

Saving Installed Packages to requirements.txt

To share your project with others or set it up on a new machine, save the installed packages in a requirements.txt file:

```
pip freeze > requirements.txt
```

This file lists all the installed packages and their versions.

Installing Packages from requirements.txt

If you clone a project with a requirements.txt file, you can install all the required packages using:

```
pip install -r requirements.txt
```

3. Structuring Python Projects

A good project structure helps in organizing your code, especially as it grows larger. Here's a basic example of how to organize a Python project:

```
my_project/
│
├── venv/                    # Virtual environment folder (not included in version control)
├── my_module/               # Your Python module/package
│   ├── __init__.py          # Marks the directory as a package
│   ├── main.py              # Main script
│   └── utils.py             # Utility functions
│
├── tests/                   # Test scripts
│   └── test_main.py         # Unit tests for main.py
│
├── requirements.txt         # Package dependencies
└── README.md                # Project documentation
```

4. Git and Version Control

Once you've set up your project and virtual environment, it's good practice to use version control with **Git** and **GitHub**.

Basic Git Workflow

1. **Initialize a Git repository**:

```
git init
```

2. **Add files**:

```
git add .
```

3. **Commit changes**:

```
git commit -m "Initial commit"
```

4. **Push to GitHub** (after setting up a remote repository):

```
git push origin main
```

Use a `.gitignore` file to ignore unnecessary files (e.g., the virtual environment) in your repository:

```
# .gitignore
venv/
__pycache__/
```

5. Advanced Topics

- **Docker**: Containerize your Python applications to ensure consistent environments across different machines.
- **CI/CD Pipelines**: Automate testing and deployment using services like GitHub Actions or Travis CI.
- **Unit Testing**: Use Python's `unittest` module or third-party frameworks like **pytest** to test your code.

Conclusion

These appendices provide a quick reference for Python syntax, methods, and advanced project setups. As your projects grow, tools like **virtual environments**, **pip**, and **Git** will become invaluable in managing dependencies and collaboration.

Keep these guides handy as you embark on more advanced Python projects, and always strive for clean, efficient, and well-organized code!

A word from the author:

Thank you for taking the time to explore **Python in Action: A Project-Based Introduction to Python Programming**! I hope the hands-on approach and practical applications have helped you strengthen your Python development skills and build confidence in your abilities.

If you found the book valuable, I'd be incredibly grateful if you could leave a review on **Amazon** or **Google Books**. Your feedback not only helps others discover the book but also supports the programming community in finding high-quality learning resources.

Don't forget to visit LearnProgramming.tips for more in-depth tutorials, resources, and tips to keep leveling up your programming skills. Your journey as a developer doesn't stop here—there's always more to learn!

Thank you for your support, and happy coding!

Impressum
Andreas Braumann, MSc
Division by Heroes e.U.
Liniengasse 48/22, 1060 Wien
Firmenbuchnummer: 506683y
GLN: 9110027158125
UID Nummer: ATU65007137
Zuständige Behörde: Magistratisches Bezirksamt für den 6. Bezirk
Unternehmensgegenstand: Webdesign
Mitglied der Wirtschaftskammer Wien
Fachgruppe Unternehmensberatung, Buchhaltung und Informationstechnologie (IT-Dienstleistung)
Berufsrecht: Gewerbeordnung: www.ris.bka.gv.at
E-Mail: info@andreas-braumann.at
Verantwortlich für den Inhalt: Andreas Braumann, MSc

www.ingramcontent.com/pod-product-compliance
Lightning Source LLC
Chambersburg PA
CBHW071058240526
45471CB00016B/2127